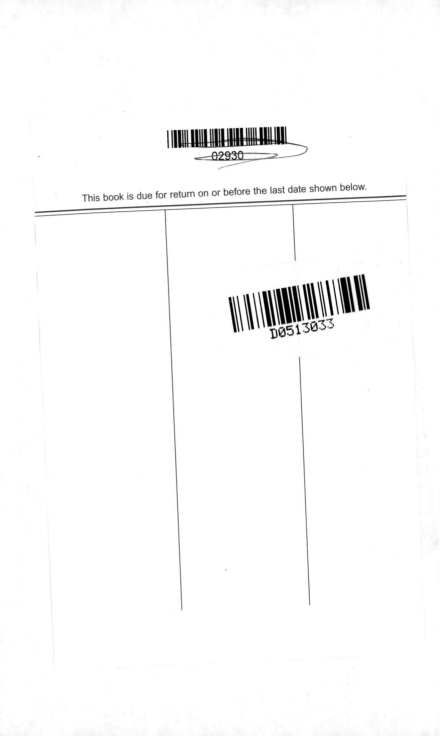

02930

This book is due for return on or before the last date shown below.

D0513033

ON THE PISTE

A bittersweet comedy

by John Godber

Warner Chappell Plays

LONDON

A Time Warner Company

First published in 1992
by Warner Chappell Plays Ltd, 129 Park Street, London W1Y 3FA.

ISBN 0 85676 128 1

Printed by Commercial Colour Press, London E7.

Author's note

The first draft of ON THE PISTE toured for a year and was
successful. However, I was never happy with the roundness of the
characters. In this version the characters are clearer and the
dialogue is much improved. As a consequence, the playing needs
the subtlety of realistic playing. The humour is not only in the
slapstick of the skiing, but in the pains of relationships.

J.H.G.

This version of ON THE PISTE was first presented at the Queen's Theatre, Hornchurch, on 29th August, 1991, with the following cast:

Chris Baxter	Paul Bown
Alison Allan	Julia Deakin
Beverley Ryan	Michelle Collins
Dave Trueman	Nick Berry
Tony Muller	Peter Birch
Melissa Grey	Celia Blaker

Directed by	Bob Tomson
Set and Costumes by	Julie Godfrey
Lighting by	Dave Horn

An earlier version of ON THE PISTE was first presented on tour by Upstart and Hull Truck Productions in 1990 with the following cast:

Chris Baxter	Paul Rider
Alison Allan	Jane Clifford
Beverley Ryan	Gillian Tompkins
Dave Trueman	Andrew Dunn
Tony Muller	Robert Hudson
Melissa Southern	Jane Bullman

Directed by	John Godber
Set and Costumes by	Robert Jones
Lighting by	Jason Taylor

The play is set in Austria, in the present day.

CHARACTERS

CHRIS BAXTER............Highly educated, very bright, witty and extremely likeable. A DJ with a local Northern radio station. A personality, but quite sensitive.

ALISON ALLAN.............Schoolteacher. Kind, attractive. Not without a strong edge. Emotional, pulsing away under the surface.

DAVE TRUEMAN..........A bit of a lad, freewheeler. Gushy, loud, cruel. Dangerous. Loves himself. Out for an easy ride.

BEV RYAN...................Effusive, kind, daffy, silly. Ultimately very honest. Vulnerable. Works in a record shop, expresses her every thought. Physically attractive.

MELISSA GREY.............Extremely confident, stunningly attractive, but beneath it all maybe quite horny. Knows the game, has probably been hurt more than the others, strong but not aggressive.

TONY MULLER.............A personality. Likeable. Very fit and effusive, easy going, but has he ulterior motives? Genuinely good fun.

ACT ONE

Scene One: A small nursery slope, Seefeld. Day.

Scene Two: The Seefelderhoff Hotel lounge. Night.

Scene Three: The Thomas lift slope, Seefeld. Day.

Scene Four: The Seefelderhoff sauna. Night.

Scene Five: The Rosschutte chair lift. The next evening.

Scene Six: The Gwanschoff mountain top. Later, the same night.

ACT TWO

Scene One: Snowy slope outside the hotel. The following night.

Scene Two: The Seefelderhoff Hotel lobby. The next day.

Scene Three: The Thomas lift slope. Seefeld. Later that day.

Scene Four: The bedroom, Seefelderhoff Hotel. Night.

Scene Five: The Thomas lift slope, Seefeld. The next day.

Scene Six: Seefelderhoff Hotel lounge/disco. A night later.

Scene Seven: A small nursery slope outside the hotel. The next day.

ACT ONE

Scene One

A large white slope with a few ferns here and there fills the space. We are in Seefeld, Austria. The time is the present. As the play opens, the stage should give the impression that we are at the foot of a mountain. Abba music plays. From upstage, TONY, *the ski instructor, enters. He snaps on his skis and skis downstage. He does a complicated cross of his skis and snaps out of them. As he does this,* MELISSA, *wearing sunglasses and the latest ski gear, enters left.* TONY *is very ebullient.*

TONY   Ar . . . so the snow is here. You have brought the snow with you, this is very good. I remember you from last year. You stay at the Seefelderhof with your husband!

MEL   Yes, that's right!

TONY   See I remember. Tony always remembers. Never forgets, yes?

MEL   Yes, so it would seem.

TONY   You are with my private school? I teach you very good skiing?

MEL   It's okay. I don't need lessons, thanks.

TONY   Oh yes, surely you must. Just a few, uh?

MEL   I don't think so. I've been skiing quite a lot since last year.

TONY   Ah very good.

MEL   Switzerland is excellent.

TONY   Ah yes.

MEL   I've been up to Davos twice. Have you ever been? It's wonderful.

TONY   Ah, Switzerland is good, but it is not so good as Austria.

MEL   It is.

TONY   No, I do not think so.

MEL   (*teasing*) Yes, it is. They have better snow.

TONY   Impossible. Austrian snow is the best snow.

MEL   Oh really?

TONY   Of course. This snow I have it brought especially for you. You will like this snow. You ski with me, I will show you some excellent runs, after my school. You tell your husband we go on the Gwanschoff . . . very good.

MEL   I don't think so.

TONY   You are scared of the Gwanschoff Mountain?

MEL   Yes I am, actually.

TONY   It is nothing.

MEL   I'll take your word for it.

TONY   You are English, yes?

MEL   Yes, that's right.

TONY   I think the English are in Europe, we must mix, yes?

MEL   I suppose . . .

TONY   I think we must, it is very important. I can speak to you in English and this is very good. But, English, Italiano, Deutch . . .

MEL   Francais?

TONY   Oui, un petit peu. But it is not important any more. I think it is important that we are all European.

MEL   I think you're right.

TONY   I have been to England.

MEL   Really?

TONY   I have been to London and Bristol.

MEL   (*only mildly interested*) Great!

TONY   My brother has been to Brighton and Hove.

MEL   Oh really!

(DAVE *and* BEV *enter carrying their skis.* ALI *and* CHRIS *shuffle behind them carrying their skis. The four of them are dressed in the height of ski fashion wear. All wear the boots, which makes it difficult to walk. They come carefully down the slope and form a half circle near* TONY.)

TONY   And so here they come. My ski school. English I think?

MEL   (*exiting*) How did you guess?

TONY   Good morning. Good morning. Please to come. Very good. English yes? Very good. You look wonderful. Welcome to Austria. My name is Tony, yes? Welcome.

          (TONY *shakes hands with the men and kisses the ladies.*)

TONY   Tony, welcome. (*Pecks* ALI's *cheek.*)

ALI   Alison.

TONY   Tony. Hello. (*Pecks* BEV.)

BEV   Hello . . . Nice to meet you. I'm Bev.

TONY   Tony . . . welcome to Seefeld. (*Shakes* DAVE's *hand.*)

DAVE   Dave. Thanks.

TONY   Tony. (*Shakes* CHRIS's *hand.*)

CHRIS   Chris, alright.

TONY   Very good, very good. At last we are all here and the morning is nearly over. We have been queuing for the skis, queuing for the lift. But now we are here, we are going to have a good time. We all look very good. We all look very sexy, yes?

BEV   Oh, hear that Dave?

TONY   I think so. I will make you the best skiers in Seefeld. With Tony it is going to be so good yes?

ALI   Yes.

TONY   (*encouraging*) We all say . . . 'Yes'!

ALL   Yes!

TONY	Very good. I can see this will be a very good holiday for you. And when you return you can say what a good teacher I am, okay? Okay. We will all have good time. Yes?
ALL	Yes.
TONY	Good.
CHRIS	Yes.
TONY	Very good. So we make to start. We all think that skiing is easy? Yes?
ALL	Yes.
TONY	No.
ALI	Oh.
TONY	I don't think so. It is very hard. Even the simple thing is very difficult. But you have a good teacher, you listen to Tony and you will learn quickly. Even the snowplough I think it is very hard. You must all be very sexy in the body, yes?
ALL	Yes.
TONY	Very sexy in the body. On your legs, very stiff. Not so easy, but we all try. We are fit yes?
BEV	I'm not fit.
CHRIS	(to BEV) Well you look it.
BEV	I get flushed going upstairs.
DAVE	I'm fit to drop, Tony.
TONY	Very good. I think you will be very fit. We are a small group. The other schools they are too big. They are all falling over like the Kops from Keystone.
BEV	You mean Keystone Kops.
TONY	I'm sorry?
BEV	You said Kops of Keystone, but you meant Keystone Kops, they're from America.
TONY	From America.

BEV	Yes, they're silent movie stars.

(A beat. TONY ignores this.)

TONY	Okay! The boots are very important, they must fit like a glove. Please now to fasten the boots. To clip the boots. Very tight. Fasten boots please. Yes.

(They all begin to clip their boots. It is very awkward. TONY goes around assisting.)

Tight, good feels tight. Yes in front of the boot, Chris very tight. Yes?

CHRIS	Yes, great thanks, no problem. Just can't get the back . . . *(He does it.)* Done it. *(Stands.)* Feels great.
TONY	Dave, good. Bev good, yes?
BEV	*(looks at her boots)* I don't think I'll be able to walk in these.
DAVE	You don't walk in them, Bev.
BEV	I know silly . . .
TONY	Alison, Gutt?
ALI	Yeah.
TONY	And so now we put on the skis. So we make the skis on the snow. Front of the boot in the front clip - snap the heel. Front of the boot in the front clip - snap the heel. So we have schnapps already and it's not even lunchtime . . . Bev, very good, but wrong way around. Feel the thighs.

(BEV feels DAVE's thighs.)

Feel your own thighs, Bev. Very good. So the boots are so tight we can lean forward, touch the front of the skis, so.

(CHRIS tries to do so, shuffles along.)

CHRIS	You okay Al?
ALI	Yeah.
CHRIS	Enjoying it?
ALI	Brilliant.

DAVE	I feel like Jean Claud Killy already.

(All now have their skis on. BEV is worried. She moves her skis along the snow.)

BEV	Tony, I think my skis are too slippery.
CHRIS	Maybe we could swap, Bev. Mine aren't slippery enough.
BEV	Do you think we should?
ALI	He's joking, Bev.
TONY	So now we make a circle. We walk around in a circle and we get used to the skis, just in a small circle.

(They begin to walk around in a small circle on the stage. BEV's ski poles hit DAVE between the legs.)

DAVE	Mind me tackle, Bev!
BEV	Sorry babe! Hi-ho, hi-ho, it's off to work we go!
TONY	Very good. Wonderful racing team.
BEV	Easy, isn't it?
CHRIS	*(affects being blind, putting his ski poles in front of him)* Penny for the blind man.
ALI	Don't be stupid.
BEV	Isn't it easy.
DAVE	We're only walking.
BEV	*(concentrating like mad)* Still easy though.
DAVE	Is this a nursery class?
CHRIS	No it's a prenatal class.
ALI	Don't make me laugh Chris, I'll fall over.
TONY	*(to stop them)* So, very good. Very good. We give ourselves a round of applause I think. Very good.

(They all applaud themselves.)

And now we go up to the slope and we ski.

(DAVE *makes a mad dash to go up the stage, but comes down backwards.*)

DAVE   Oh yes, what about this?

BEV   Wrong way, babe . . .

TONY   Very good Dave, but like a bull in a shop of china. (*Side stepping.*) So now we make to go side-stepping up the hill. Skis into the hill. Little steps, into the hill. And then move across, make one side of the ski into the hill and then bring the knees together and we schuss down the hill. Skis turned inwards. And this we call . . .

CHRIS   The snowplough?

TONY   Are yes, very good Chris. The snowplough. And so we schuss down the hill.

(*They all begin to side-step into the hill. DAVE leads, then BEV, then ALI, and then a very clumsy CHRIS. As they all side-step, DAVE slips and this means BEV slips, but remains standing, and all of them laugh at this minor error.*)

Very good. Bon Gutt. Excellent.

(DAVE *is now making to centre stage. He positions himself upstage centre. Adjusts his skis and schusses downstage. He screams. But is successful.*)

DAVE   Arrrrrhhhh . . .

BEV   Brilliant. Well done, babe.

TONY   Very good. And so to you, Bev. Spread your legs.

DAVE   Come on, Bev - you never had any trouble before!

BEV   Oh, don't!

(DAVE *now makes his way back to the side-stepping side of the stage. TONY looks on from downstage right as BEV, agonisingly slowly, makes her way stage centre. She makes great play of putting the side of the ski into the snow, and then places her knees very close together. She looks almost deformed. Slowly, almost inordinately, she moves down the stage. The movement should be as slow as possible. Throughout this she concentrates like Franz Klammer. All the*) *others watch her in disbelief. At the bottom of the slope, she stops and looks to* TONY *for some reward.*)

TONY Very good.

(*He applauds her, they all applaud her, and she applauds herself.*)

BEV It's fantastic.

TONY So, Alison.

(BEV *now moves aside and back to the side-stepping hill while* ALI *moves centre stage. She has clearly skied before and she makes a passable snowplough turn and stop. All applaud.*)

Ah so . . . very good Alison. You have skied before?

ALI A little bit.

TONY Very good. Excellent. Ah, this is my best class all year. Very good school. (*To* CHRIS.) So, Cliff, for you the snowplough.

CHRIS Chris.

TONY Excuse me - Chris, for you the snowplough.

(CHRIS *is now making his way across to stage centre. He is pathetic. When he is in position, he makes a crouching stance like a downhill racer. He takes his time, making very crouching movements. Suddenly he is off, and falls over downstage centre. He laughs.*)

No-no-no-no-no, lean forward more Chris.

(*They all applaud him.*)

CHRIS (*laughing, but hurt*) What about that, then?

DAVE Nice one, Chris.

CHRIS Brilliant, eh?

ALI Fantastic.

CHRIS I'm going to love this, I can see that.

TONY So we try once again. You okay, Chris?

CHRIS I'm fine, no problem.

ALI	. . . Can you get up?
CHRIS	Just about.

(CHRIS *cannot get up. He finds it funny, so should we. He is rolling around, trying to get on his feet.*)

BEV	You alright, Chris?
CHRIS	Fine yeah, no problem. I'll be back up in no time at all. If I could just get, my weight up here . . . I'd be laughing. (*He is struggling like mad.*)
BEV	I didn't realise it would be so easy.
CHRIS	Oh this is great. Ha-ha, look at this . . . (*Still stuck.*)
TONY	(*coming over to* CHRIS, *helping him up*) Here we go.
CHRIS	(*he is up, but not stable*) Great, thanks. Ha-ha . . . brilliant. It's great.
TONY	We all make falls, it is okay. Are you okay?
CHRIS	Yeah I'm great.
TONY	Again please, very carefully we make, go snowplough.

(*They begin to side-step. Once more* DAVE *is already moving at the top.* BEV *is hurriedly ready for another go.* ALI, *and then* CHRIS, *side-step.* TONY *watches.* DAVE *comes down the hill. Screams.*)

DAVE	Brilliantttttt!
ALI	Well done.
TONY	Very good.

(*He moves out of the way to reveal* BEV, *who moves even slower this time. Silence as we see her come down the mountain. At the bottom she looks at* TONY.)

Excellent.

DAVE	Don't go too fast Bev, you'll create a wind tunnel.
BEV	Don't be silly, I won't . . .

(BEV *moves out of the way and* ALI *comes down once more. Another excellent snowplough.*)

TONY	Alison, very good, very good.
BEV	(*to* ALI) You're good.
ALI	I'm a bit rusty.

(CHRIS *has now moved centre stage, however he is somehow facing the wrong way. He has his back to the audience.*)

TONY	No no, this way Chris.
CHRIS	Yeah I know, I'm on my way.

(*Slowly* CHRIS *tries to turn around, but it's hard. Then he decides to make small jumps in a circle with his skis together. Suddenly he is facing the right way.*)

ALI	Concentrate.
CHRIS	I am.
ALI	Concentrate on your skis.
CHRIS	I am . . . hey don't watch me, you'll put me off. Close your eyes. You're putting me off.
BEV	I'm not, am I?
DAVE	Come on Eddie the Eagle, show us what you're made of.
CHRIS	Stand by . . . I might come down so quick, I'll take the lot of you with me.
TONY	Relax Chris. Relax.
CHRIS	Stand back, here I come . . .

(CHRIS *begins to schuss down, he does a perfect snowplough. They all applaud.* CHRIS *is delighted.*)

What about that then?

TONY	Very good style.
CHRIS	A piece of cake.

(*As* CHRIS *speaks he simply falls over sideways and hits the floor.*)

DAVE	That was brilliant.

CHRIS	Yeah, I'm good at falling over. I could do this all day.
	(CHRIS *is prostrate on stage.*)
BEV	Isn't it cold?
DAVE	What did you expect?
CHRIS	If I could just get my weight up here . . .
ALI	Do you want help?
CHRIS	(*struggling*) No no, I'm okay . . .
TONY	Relax, Chris . . .
CHRIS	I couldn't be much more relaxed . . .
TONY	Dig in the poles.
	(ALI *makes a move to* CHRIS, *pulls him up and they are together, close.* BEV *and* DAVE *are also close.*)
ALI	Up we come. Yeah?
CHRIS	Thanks Al.
ALI	Okay?
CHRIS	Just about.
ALI	You had it.
CHRIS	I know.
ALI	Showing off, as usual.
CHRIS	I had it, didn't I? I had it.
ALI	Yes, perfect.
CHRIS	No problem.
DAVE	You had it there Chris.
TONY	Very good. You are all my top students.
BEV	Isn't it cold? Give us a cuddle Dave.
DAVE	Bev, I'm sweating like a pig.
	(DAVE *cuddles* BEV *upstage.* TONY *watches.*)
TONY	Ah, very good. We are all in love. Yes?

BEV	Yes.
ALI	Cold?
CHRIS	Freezing!
ALI	Good fun though?
CHRIS	Oh yeah. Brilliant fun.
ALI	You look great.
CHRIS	Do I?
ALI	Yeah.
CHRIS	I'm the only man in Seefeld with a blue face.
ALI	You're trying too hard. Do what Tony says. Just go limp.
CHRIS	(*obvious*) Hey none of that?
ALI	Come here. Give us a kiss, blue nose.

(CHRIS *kisses* ALI.)

Give me a proper kiss.

(*He kisses her deeper. Longer.*)

That's better.

TONY	(*musing*) Ah yes we are in love. This is Austria, it is very romantic, everyone falls in love in Austria. Many people come, they are not in love, but for two days in Seefeld and they are in love.
BEV	Oh that's nice.
TONY	They fall in love in Seefeld and I think they are in love for the rest of their lives.
BEV	Great.
TONY	After the skiing you will have the sauna and swim. It will make you all feel very sexy, believe me. I know, I do this everyday.
ALI	We'll take your word for it.
TONY	But we talk too much and we get cold in the bones, and soon we are like Stone Hindge.

BEV	Stonehenge.
TONY	Very good, yes. Stone Henge. I know this, I have been . . .
BEV	Tony, can we go for lunch now because I'm getting really cold, aren't I babe?
DAVE	Yeah she is.
TONY	You are very cold?
BEV	Freezing. Aren't you cold, Chris?
CHRIS	I don't know, I can't feel anything.
TONY	It is not good to go back, but if you are cold I must let you go back to the hotel. Yes.
BEV	Oh yes, yes! (*To* ALI.) If I get too cold Ali, I get chest pains.
ALI	Oh right. Better be safe than sorry.
BEV	Yeah. Come on Dave. Let's go back and get warm. (BEV *knocks* CHRIS *over with her skis.*) Oh, sorry, Chris!
CHRIS	It's alright.
DAVE	Okay. See you later.
CHRIS	You betcha . . .
DAVE	Probably do a black run after lunch. Cheers, Tony, mate.
TONY	And after lunch we do some of this for the confidence.
	(*He snowploughs down the slope with his poles behind his knees.* BEV *and* DAVE *exit.*)
DAVE	(*exiting*) I'll see you later.
CHRIS	Part-timers. It's just us then, Tony. So what's next?
TONY	Very good. So Chris, for you another snowplough.
CHRIS	Another?
TONY	I think. Yes.

CHRIS	Brilliant. Watch this.

(CHRIS *begins to side-step up the hill,* TONY *crosses to* ALI.)

TONY	He is very determined?
ALI	Oh yes, if he says he'll do something, he'll do it.
TONY	It will come for him, he will be very good.
ALI	Do you think so?
TONY	Oh yes, he will be very good. So remember Chris, lean forward.
CHRIS	Lean forward, Chris!

(CHRIS *is now upstage centre, and ready to schuss down, but he makes a complete mess of it. He falls forward onto the poles, his hands slide down the poles and as he does this his skis do the splits behind him.* ALI *laughs,* CHRIS *laughs.* TONY *goes to him.* CHRIS *falls to the snow.*)

TONY	(*encouraging*) No no no, Chris, you lean forward, it is no good. Lean backwards yes! Then you will be very good. I tell Alison that you will be good and then you fall, this is not good. Make me look bad.
CHRIS	I think I know what I'm doing wrong.
ALI	Yeah, you're supposed to stay stood up.

(CHRIS *sits in the snow.*)

CHRIS	At least I haven't broken anything.
ALI	Yet.
CHRIS	(*lightly*) Oh thank you very much!
TONY	Tomorrow I will take you higher up the mountain. And before we all go back I think we will all ski down the mountain. Even Bev I think.
CHRIS	Even me?
TONY	You Chris are star pupil.
ALI	Can you ski down that?

(*She points into the audience. The mountain is a monster.*)

TONY   I can ski that one backwards on one leg with my
            eyes closed.

CHRIS   Modesty not one of your virtues, is it Tony?

TONY   Please?

ALI   (*still mountain gazing*) What a mountain.

TONY   This mountain is the Rosschutte. It is easy for me.
            This mountain . . . (*He gestures to another.*) . . . is a
            monster. It is the Gwanschoff. Not so easy. But for
            me I am three years champion on the Gwanschoff.

CHRIS   (*looking*) People ski down that? Give over.

TONY   In Calgary I win Bronze medal. Now so-so. Maybe
            not so hot. But I still train very hard. Okay. So this
            morning I make it easy for you. We make an end
            now. I go for lunch now, very good restaurant. You
            eat too, yes? You like, yes?

ALI   Yes.

TONY   You enjoy.

ALI   Yeah . . .

CHRIS   . . . great thanks.

TONY   Good. Alison you are excellent. You are star pupil.

CHRIS   I thought I was the star pupil?

TONY   I make a joke for you, Chris.

CHRIS   (*not hurt*) Thanks a lot.

TONY   (*ready to depart*) You stay or you go?

CHRIS   Stay. More practice.

TONY   Very good. Good bye. Good practice.

            (*Without more to do,* TONY *departs.* CHRIS *watches
            him go. Silence.*)

CHRIS   What a prat.

ALI   Who?

CHRIS   Me.

ALI   Why?

CHRIS	I don't know . . .
ALI	You've done alright.
CHRIS	Come on Al?
ALI	You have.
CHRIS	Tell the truth.
ALI	You have.
CHRIS	Weren't you embarrassed by me?
ALI	No.
CHRIS	Tell the truth.
ALI	Honest. You did okay. You can't expect to be good at everything.
CHRIS	Why not, you are.
ALI	You did alright, for an old man.
CHRIS	That's just what I want to hear.
ALI	Well you did.
CHRIS	Did I?
ALI	I think so. Let's not practice. I'm freezing.
CHRIS	Come here, give us another kiss then.
	(ALI *comes to* CHRIS. *They kiss, he holds her as best you can in ski gear.*)
	See, we can have a good time can't we?
ALI	'Course we can. Don't you think it's romantic?
CHRIS	It ought to be for the money we've paid.
ALI	Oh it is though, don't you think?
CHRIS	(*easy*) No.
ALI	You do.
CHRIS	I don't.
ALI	Yes you do.

CHRIS	Do I?
ALI	You know you do
CHRIS	Oh yeah . . . isn't it romantic?
ALI	I knew you'd love skiing. You didn't want to come and now you're hooked.
CHRIS	I wouldn't go that far.
ALI	You know some couples don't make the effort when they've been together for as long as we have.
CHRIS	(*mock*) Really?
ALI	They just drift on, nothing new comes into their life. They get into a rut.

(ALI *comes close to* CHRIS.)

CHRIS	(*lost, musing*) Yeah.
ALI	I wonder why we've stayed together for so long?
CHRIS	It's me. I don't like changes.
ALI	(*hurt*) Don't . . .
CHRIS	(*true, but covering*) I'm only joking. Don't be so touchy.
ALI	Me touchy? Listen whose talking, you can't say two words to you without you're up in arms.
CHRIS	(*acting it*) Hey hey now . . . you promised . . . On holiday . . . what did you promise?
ALI	No arguing.
CHRIS	Remember - no points scoring.

(*A pause. They are getting cold.*)

ALI	Cold?
CHRIS	Mmmmm.
ALI	So what do you fancy?
CHRIS	A magic carpet to take me back to the hotel. Wooosh. (*He mimes the carpet.*)

ALI	I mean when we get back?
CHRIS	Sauerkraut.
ALI	And then what?
CHRIS	A cup of coffee.
ALI	After that?
CHRIS	I'm too tired. Got to save meself for this afternoon.
ALI	(*teasing*) No you're not.
CHRIS	(*pathetic*) I am.
ALI	You're not.
CHRIS	Al, I'm knackered.
ALI	I've got some oil, I'll give you a massage.
CHRIS	I'm really tired.
ALI	Did you hear me?
CHRIS	What sort of massage?
ALI	An all-over massage.
CHRIS	Brilliant . . . I'll just have one more go . . . (*He begins to side-step up the mountain.*)
ALI	Chris . . . Chris . . . Come on . . .
CHRIS	Just one more go . . . just one more.
ALI	Chris? Chris? Chris? It's lunch time, Chris.
CHRIS	Just one more, Ali . . .
ALI	You're like a kid . . .
CHRIS	I know - it's brilliant.
ALI	Come on then, Franz Klammer, get on with it.
	(CHRIS *side-steps.* ALI *watches. Abba plays and the lights fade.*)

Scene Two

*The Hotel Seefelderhof. Night. A glowing fire. Pine everywhere,
the atmosphere, warm and luxuriating.* BEV, *wearing Après ski
clothes, and* DAVE, *wearing trendy tracksuit and trainers, lounge
near the fire.* DAVE *has a large stein of lager,* BEV *is drinking a
glass of white wine. They are close together.* DAVE *is sat behind*
BEV *and is fondling her, their horseplay having sexual under and
overtones.* BEV *is giggling as* DAVE *fondles her stomach.*

BEV   (*laughing*) Don't!

DAVE   Come here . . .

BEV   Oh . . .

DAVE   Grrr . . .

BEV   Gerroff me . . .

DAVE   Come here let me ravish you!

BEV   Not here, babe!

DAVE   (*wrestling*) Come here, give us a kiss.

BEV   Oh you sex maniac.

               (BEV *and* DAVE *have one long kiss.* DAVE *fondles
               her, she giggles and pulls away.*)

DAVE   Warm?

BEV   I am now.

DAVE   I hope the beds are well made Bev.

BEV   You're awful.

DAVE   No I'm not.

BEV   I thought you were really good today, babe. I was
               proud of you.

DAVE   You were? I was proud of you.

BEV   Was I?

DAVE   Yeah, I thought you were great.

BEV   Oh, it's just like the brochure isn't it?

DAVE   Suppose . . . it is, yeah . . .

           (BEV *has a moment's thought, then dreamily*.)

BEV   Daaaaaavee?

DAVE   (*copying her tone*) Whaaaaatttt?

BEV   Do you know what I've been thinking?

DAVE   Noooooo.

BEV   Don't you think it would be great if you came and
           moved in?

           (DAVE *is shocked, but plays it cool*.)

DAVE   Eh?

BEV   Yeah, you know, we'd both save money and all that.
           You could come and move into my flat. Don't you
           think it would be a good idea?

DAVE   Well yeah.

BEV   Well then, lets do it babe, you move in with me, it'd
           be brilliant.

DAVE   Well. I mean, I dunno.

BEV   Why?

DAVE   Dunno.

BEV   Don't you love me?

DAVE   'Course I do.

BEV   Do you?

DAVE   Yeah.

BEV   Do you honestly?

DAVE   I love being with you Bev.

BEV   It's not the same.

DAVE   'Course it is.

BEV   It's not.

DAVE   It is.

BEV   Is it?

DAVE   Yeah. It's just that we've only known each other . . .
            how long is it?

BEV   Six months.

DAVE   That long?

BEV   Oh it's been brilliant babe, hasn't it?

DAVE   Well yeah . . .

BEV   Well, and it's right isn't it?

DAVE   Well it feels right . . .

BEV   So?

            (DAVE *feels uncomfortable, decides to divert.*)

DAVE   I dunno babe, I mean I've always been a loner,
            know what I mean? I'll have to think about it. I mean,
            in any case I'll have to ask Kevin.

BEV   Oh, Kevin'll love it Dave. Ask him.

DAVE   No. Leave him, Bev.

BEV   I'll ask him. (*Changes her vocal tone as if she is
            talking to a five year old boy.*) Kevin? Kev? Does he
            want to come and stay with his Aunty Bev?

DAVE   (*as a five year old boy*) I'm tired.

BEV   Are you tired?

DAVE   (*Kev*) Yeah.

BEV   Has the skiing tired you out?

DAVE   (*Kev*) Yeah. I'm tired out.

BEV   Are you enjoying Austria?

DAVE   (*Kev*) Yeah it's absolutely fantastic in Austria. I like it
            because there's lots of snow, and nice fings to eat
            and lots of nice ladies in ski pants.

BEV   Does he love his Aunty Bev?

DAVE   (*Kev*) Yes, he loves being with his Aunty Bev, he
           thinks it's fantastic.

BEV   Does he?

DAVE   (*Kev*) Yes he does.

BEV   Is he going to think about him and his Uncle Dave
           moving into Aunty Bev's flat?

DAVE   (*Kev*) Yeah yeah, he says he'll think about it, but at
           the moment he's too tired to think about it.

BEV   Is he?

DAVE   (*Kev*) Yes he is.

BEV   I bet he is.

DAVE   (*Kev*) He's drifting off to sleep. (DAVE *snores as
           Kevin, and then speaks as* DAVE.) He must have
           nodded off to sleep, Bev.

BEV   Bless him.

           (MELISSA *enters from outside. She is wrapped up in
           full gear, she appears slightly upset. Lost, maybe.*)

DAVE   I don't want to waken him Bev, so I'll have another
           drink and let him sleep.

           (DAVE *sips his lager.* BEV *addresses* MELISSA.)

BEV   Hiya . . .

MEL   (*only half polite*) Hi . . .

BEV   Cold . . .

MEL   Outside?

BEV   Yes. Cold?

MEL   Very. Freezing. Minus three I think.

BEV   We decided to stay in.

MEL   (*not interested*) Really?

BEV   I don't like the cold weather. I've got a bad chest.

MEL   Well I should stay indoors. Minus three I think.

DAVE	Brass monkey weather.
MEL	Sorry?
BEV	Dave! Take no notice of him, he's rude.
MEL	What did he say?
DAVE	(*idle, loud*) I said it's brass monkey weather, cold enough to freeze your truffles off. That is if you've got any truffles to freeze off.
MEL	(*a beat*) Oh.
BEV	(*light*) Take no notice of him.
MEL	Oh, right.
BEV	I'm Bev. Who are you?
MEL	(*taken aback*) Oh well hermmm . . . I'm ermmmm . . .
DAVE	You've got her there Bev - she doesn't know her own name . . .
MEL	Mel. Melissa actually. Hi. Sorry. I'm, well . . . nice to meet you.
BEV	This is Dave.
MEL	Oh right. Hi.
DAVE	Want a drink Melissa? Warm you up a bit?
MEL	No . . . I'm fine thanks.
DAVE	Sure?
MEL	What? Yes. Sorry.
BEV	Are you alright?
	(BEV *senses all is not right.*)
MEL	Why? Don't I . . .
BEV	You look upset . . .
MEL	No, no I'm fine. I'm fine, really.
BEV	Are you sure?
MEL	(*sharp*) Of course.

BEV	Oh. It's just that your cheeks? It must be the cold. I thought it looked like you'd been crying?
MEL	Must be the cold.
BEV	Must be.
DAVE	(*brash*) You come in a group then Melissa?
MEL	No I haven't actually, I'm by myself. I erm, well, I just came away for a few days just to get away for a while really. You know? I love skiing, so I thought it would be a nice little break.
DAVE	Oh nice one.
BEV	(*eager*) If you feel lonely you could come with us you know, if you feel like you want a bit of a laugh. Can't she babe? You can come in our group. Be great that wouldn't it Dave?
DAVE	Yeah . . . great stuff.
MEL	Well I'll think about it.
DAVE	It's an offer you can't refuse.
MEL	Really?
BEV	Can you ski?
MEL	A little bit.
DAVE	She's probably an expert, aren't you?
MEL	Not quite.
BEV	We can snowplough. Dave's brilliant. He's a natural, aren't you?
DAVE	Beginners luck.
BEV	Oh come with us Mel, if you're feeling a bit low come out with us, we have a laugh, don't we Dave!
	(*As* BEV *speaks*, CHRIS *enters. He is dressed Après ski and comes near to* MELISSA.)
DAVE	Speaking of which.
CHRIS	Evening all. Where is everybody?

BEV	Hiya Chris. Chris this is Melissa, she might be coming out with us tomorrow.
CHRIS	Hello. (*Shakes* MELISSA's *hand*.) Oh, cold hand warm heart.
BEV	Minus three.
DAVE	Everyone else is in bed. They're all shagged out.
CHRIS	Isn't that what they say?
MEL	I don't know.
DAVE	Are you stiff, Chris?
CHRIS	Not yet, are you?
DAVE	No way.
MEL	Anyway. I must go. Nice to meet you all.
BEV	See you at breakfast, Mel?
MEL	I should think so. Good night. Good night.
CHRIS	Night.
DAVE	Bye.

(MEL *goes.* DAVE *and* CHRIS *watch as she does.* BEV *is oblivious to this.*)

BEV	She's nice babe, don't you think? Really pretty.
DAVE	(*liar*) No. Plastic.
CHRIS	It's warm in here.
BEV	Minus three outside, Chris.
CHRIS	So I heard.
DAVE	So how's Chris?
CHRIS	Fine. Great.
DAVE	No problems?
CHRIS	None that I can think of.
DAVE	Well there's a lucky man. Took a few tumbles today though Chris. Talk about arse over tit, you did it. It looked like you were trying to kill yourself.

CHRIS   (*playing along*) It was all a show Dave, just to make
            you feel good. Tomorrow, schooosss, you just see.
            I've been putting some extra practice in.

DAVE   Lulling us into a false sense of security?

CHRIS   That's it. Anyone fancy a drink?

BEV   No thanks.

CHRIS   Dave, another bucket of lager?

DAVE   No, cheers . . . where's the other half?

CHRIS   Bed.

BEV   Is she tired?

CHRIS   Wiped out. I think it must be the fresh air.

DAVE   Best place to be.

CHRIS   You two look cosy.

BEV   We are.

DAVE   Don't want to join us do you? The three of us?

CHRIS   (*frightened it's for real*) No . . . I . . .

DAVE   Only joking . . . I've heard about these skiing
            holidays.

BEV   What is it that you do Chris?

CHRIS   Eh?

BEV   What job do you do?

CHRIS   Oh it's a bit of a funny job really. I er . . . work for a
            radio station. Afternoons, easy listening sort of thing.
            I'm a Disc Jockey.

BEV   Oh isn't that weird?

CHRIS   Is it?

DAVE   She works in a record shop.

CHRIS   Oh right. Great. Is it good? Is it interesting I mean?
            You know, selling records?

BEV	No, it's boring, really.
CHRIS	How about you, Dave?
DAVE	Motors.
CHRIS	Oh, right.
DAVE	Disc jockey, eh?
CHRIS	Yeah, and I do a bit of freelance work doing voice overs for tele, you know, that sort of thing. It's only a small station in the North, nothing special . . . "Chris Baxter's Lazy Hour" . . . And we do 'phone-ins', you know the sort of thing?
BEV	Have you done anything we might know?
CHRIS	What?
BEV	The adverts.
CHRIS	Well, no . . . I don't know, really.
BEV	Are you famous?
CHRIS	No.
BEV	What have you done then?
CHRIS	Well nothing, really.
BEV	Oh come on, tell us what you've done.
DAVE	Yeah.
CHRIS	Well . . . last year I did, what was it, I did a yoghurt and a Paint Seal advert, and one for selling off water.
DAVE	Dodgy . . .
CHRIS	Good money, but I don't talk about it.
DAVE	Fair point.
BEV	I saw that one, that water one. That was you was it?
CHRIS	Well, it was my voice.
BEV	I thought that was good. Did you babe?
CHRIS	And I've done one that is well known but it's a secret, I don't tell anyone about that.

BEV	Tell us . . . (*She begins to drift, tired.*)
CHRIS	I can't. It's a secret.
BEV	(*disappointed*) Oh.
DAVE	You're not a Tetley tea bag are you?
CHRIS	The chance would be a fine thing.
BEV	I've never met anyone famous before.
CHRIS	I'm not famous.
DAVE	He's not famous is he, he's only the voice.
CHRIS	(*hurt*) That's right. I'm only the voice.
BEV	We don't sell many Easy Listening records, they're more for the older end. We sell mostly pop.
CHRIS	Oh right.
DAVE	He sounds like a Tetley tea bag to me. Does he sound like a Tetley tea bag to you Bev?
BEV	He does a bit, yeah.
CHRIS	Well I'm not.
DAVE	You're not a McCain Oven Chip are you?
CHRIS	Sorry.
	(BEV *seems incredibly tired and is nodding off.* DAVE *notices.* CHRIS *looks on.*)
DAVE	Tired, Bev . . . tired? Is she tired eh, is she tired?
BEV	Yeah.
DAVE	Time for bed?
BEV	Yeah.
DAVE	Kevin's wakening up, Bev.
BEV	Is he?
DAVE	He wants to play, Bev.
BEV	(*half excited*) Oh no.

DAVE   Yeah he wants to play. Don't you Kev? (*Kev.*) Yeah, I want to play . . . I want to play with my Aunty Bev.

BEV   (*coming round*) I know what he wants to play and it's not I Spy, is it Kevin?

DAVE   (*Kev*) No it's not. He wants to play naughty boys.

BEV   (*standing*) Come on then. Let's have you. Were you like this with Ali, Chris?

            (DAVE *stands, finishes off his lager and grabs* BEV. *They are about to depart.*)

CHRIS   (*liar*) Exactly the same.

BEV   See you at breakfast, Chris?

CHRIS   Yeah.

DAVE   See you Chris. Cheers.

BEV   'Night, Chris.

            (DAVE *and* BEV *exit.*)

CHRIS   'Night . . . (*A beat.*) Sleep tight. The three of you.

            (*We hear* BEV *and* DAVE *climbing the stairs off stage, a German voice bids them "Guten Nacht". It is the voice of the hotelier.* DAVE *responds with a "good nach". The lights of the hotel lounge are switched off.* CHRIS *is seated. Only the glow of the fire, and the practicals light him. The mood shifts. It is sombre. Silence.*)

            I can remember all that Ali, can you? The togetherness? All the good times. Did we ever have any good times, Al? Or has it always been the same. You bitch at me I score one back at you? I can't remember if we ever had good times. (*Easily shifting focus.*) Yes caller on line two can I help you? (*No vocal change.*) "Yes Chris, its Chris Baxter here." Hello Chris, what can I do you for? "Well Chris, I've known this woman for ten years, met her at a gig at her college, and we've lived together for seven years and it's just a game now. What do you think I should do?"

            (*Silence.*)

I think you should play the next record Chris. Keep away from the advice, and play the next record.

(*Silence.* CHRIS *stands. He is extremely stiff, can hardly stand up straight. Stretches. 'I Have A Dream', by Abba plays. Lights fade.*)

Scene Three

We are back on the piste. However we are now higher up the slope. This may be indicated by more trees filling in the side of the stage. TONY *skis down from top stage left to downstage right. As he does this,* MELISSA *enters and skis from upstage left to downstage right. They both clip off their skis.*

TONY   So today you are with my school, this is very good.

MEL   I was press-ganged at breakfast.

TONY   Your husband is on the mountain, yes?

MEL   (*to herself*) He might as well be.

TONY   Please?

MEL   He's not here. He didn't come.

TONY   This is very bad for you.

MEL   I can live with it.

TONY   I feel very sorry for you. You are all alone at night in the hotel. Maybe tonight I will come and sleep with you. You will not be so lonely.

MEL   Oh really?

TONY   I only joke. I make you smile see? You are with my group, we can smile. They are nice people I think?

MEL   They're okay.

TONY   If you are lonely I will show you things in Seefeld.

MEL   I'm sure you would.

TONY   Ah no please, I am not coming on with you. I think you may like to talk, okay? Maybe not. I can talk you see. We can talk.

MEL   Well, I'll think about it.

TONY   I think your husband, he must be crazy in the head.
            He should be here. You are too beautiful to be alone
            in Seefeld. It is for couples I think?

MEL   That makes me feel better.

TONY   I think perhaps he is a very busy man.

MEL   Very busy.

TONY   Ah so. I am also very busy.

            (BEV, ALI *and* DAVE *enter from the back of the stage,
            all of them stiff but none of them willing to admit it.*
            BEV *is extremely stiff and moves almost like a puppet.*
            CHRIS *has not yet appeared.* DAVE *and* ALI *come
            downstage first. They are not skiing, but walking with
            great care.*)

            Ah see very good snow here. We come on the
            Thomas T-bar, yes. It was good? You are all very
            good, Yes?

ALL   (*muted*) Yes.

TONY   What do you think to my racing team?

MEL   Fantastic.

TONY   We are all feeling a little stiff this morning, yes?

ALI   Yes.

DAVE   No, I'm fine.

BEV   I'm a bit stiff Tony. All my thighs are stiff. I got on
            the loo this morning and I couldn't make my legs
            move.

DAVE   I had to pull her off.

BEV   It took me twenty minutes to get out of bed. I feel
            like a Muppet.

TONY   A Muppet? Miss Piggy. Ah yes. Yes good.

            (CHRIS *enters on his skis, upstage left.*)

CHRIS   Morning, everyone. Hey Al, I've just skied from the
            T-bar.

ALI   Well done.

DAVE   How do you feel this morning, Chris? Stiff?

CHRIS   No. Look out, here I come. Watch this, Tony.

TONY   Okay Chris, you come, I can see if you are ready for
           Austrian Olympic team.

CHRIS   I don't know about that.

BEV   Come on Chris, let's see what you're made of.

CHRIS   No, you're putting me off. Don't watch me.

ALI   Come on, get on with it.

CHRIS   Okay . . . Here we go.

           (CHRIS *skis downstage centre but it is a mistake. He
           falls all over, and hits the deck with a bump.*)

           Shit. I had it.

           (*A beat.*)

BEV   You might be better with a ski stuck to your bum,
           Chris.

ALI   Good idea, Bev.

CHRIS   I had it, honest.

DAVE   Oh yeah? Tell us another.

ALI   I believe you, love.

CHRIS   Thanks Al. I had it honest. I was amazing.

DAVE   Hey Chris, a word of advice, don't ever do a skiing
           advert. You're crap.

CHRIS   Thanks Dave. I'll try and remember that.

TONY   Still Chris, in the head, relax, knees together, yes?

CHRIS   Yes. But I'm getting better . . . Yes?

TONY   Yes, you have the guts of the racer. This is very
           good. Much determination. But.

           (CHRIS *is now back on his feet.* TONY *addresses the
           group.*)

TONY	So we get back our breath and then you all follow Tony down around the back of the Thomas lift. It is very easy. You all follow me and I look like a good teacher. Yes?
ALL	Yes.
TONY	So. I see my friend in the lift, and then we go. Alison I show you very good restaurant from here. You want to see, Maybe then for you and Chris romantic meal. It is the brother of my father.
ALI	Oh great. Chris, there's a restaurant in the hills.
TONY	Come I show you. Chris, it is okay?
CHRIS	Yeah. Do what you want Tony. (*Laughs.*)
	(ALI *and* TONY *move upstage, maybe even off.* MEL *and* CHRIS *look out towards the audience.* BEV *is near* DAVE.)
BEV	Is Kevin enjoying it?
DAVE	(*Kev*) Yeah, he finks it's brilliant. He loves all the beautiful scenery. It's great being in Austria.
BEV	He's been a naughty boy he has, Chris. He was doing some naughty things last night, wasn't he?
DAVE	(*Kev*) Yes he was. He was playing with his widgey, wasn't he?
BEV	What have I told you about language like that? Now give me a kiss.
	(DAVE *kisses* BEV.)
	Oh, isn't he brilliant?
CHRIS	Well, he's not my type.
BEV	Oh he is, though. Don't you think he's funny, Mel?
	(MEL *says nothing, just smiles.*)
DAVE	What do you think of the view, Mel?
MEL	Not bad.
DAVE	Not bad?

MEL	Wait till you get up on the Gwanschoff. It'll take your breath away.
BEV	Have you been up there?
MEL	Yes. It's wonderful. There's a Tyrolean restaurant, no doubt Tony will insist you go there. It's part of the tourist trap.
DAVE	You like Europe, then.
MEL	Well let's face it, England has become a nation of amusement arcades and theme pubs. If we had this scenery in England it would be in a leisure park.
BEV	Oh, I like England.
CHRIS	Where do you live Melissa?
MEL	I've got a place in London and a flat in Paris.
BEV	I love Paris. So romantic.
CHRIS	(*reacting to* MEL) Very nice.
MEL	It's nothing grand Chris, just a little flat.
CHRIS	It's a little flat more than I've got.
MEL	(*easily*) You're not jealous are you?
CHRIS	Why, have I gone green? I was blue yesterday.
	(*Cut across this as* TONY *and* ALI *return. They come from upstage.*)
ALI	There's a great restaurant Chris, it's just tucked away. It's only tiny. They do pizzas and stuff.
CHRIS	Yeah?
ALI	Looks fantastic.
CHRIS	We can try it one night.
ALI	You can get a sleigh ride and ride up. Sounds brilliant. Yeah?
CHRIS	Yeah.
TONY	(*at the top of the slope*) So now we all go together. Yes?

ALL	Yes.
TONY	Okay we go. Careful across the top here, very icy and then after we will ski. (TONY *exits upstage right.* BEV *moves to follow him.*)
BEV	I might lock myself in a wardrobe tomorrow. I can't take another day of this. (*She tracks off.*)
ALI	You coming Chris?
CHRIS	In a minute. I might ski down on my bum. Bum-skiing is all the rage in Canada, apparently.
ALI	Do you want me to wait?
CHRIS	No it's okay, I'll be alright. You go. I'll catch you up.
ALI	See you at the bottom.

(ALI *is making to exit.* MEL *also moves upstage.*)

MEL	No one wants to race, do they?
DAVE	Are you joking?
CHRIS	I'd love to. Maybe at the end of the week.
DAVE	I'd fall arse over tit.
MEL	Oh I'd like to see that.
DAVE	I bet you would.
MEL	See you later.
DAVE	Yeah.
CHRIS	Cheers.

(MEL *exits.* CHRIS *and* DAVE *stand together. Silence.*)

DAVE	You think you're going to master it?
CHRIS	What?
DAVE	Those ninety degree turns?
CHRIS	Yeah, looks easy though.

(DAVE *begins to attempt a ninety degree turn, but messes it up.*)

DAVE	Is that it?

36 ACT ONE

CHRIS	Make a wish, Dave . . .
DAVE	Yeah, very funny Chris, mate . . . Ohh, ah . . . Now what?
CHRIS	Dunno. Looks like you're stuck there, Dave.
DAVE	(*finally making the turn*) Yeeeeeees! What about that? Have a go, Chris.
CHRIS	I think I'll give that one a miss, Dave. It looks unhealthy.
DAVE	Oh yes. I'll tell you something. I don't know about you but all this fresh air is getting to me.
CHRIS	Tiring you is it?
DAVE	No. The opposite. I feel as frisky as hell.
CHRIS	Yeah, well keep your distance.
DAVE	(*doing another successful turn*) Don't worry.
CHRIS	What do you think to who-is-it?
DAVE	Who?
CHRIS	. . . Melissa.
DAVE	It's a mouthful, isn't it?
CHRIS	Not half.
DAVE	She's not in our league, mate.
CHRIS	You never know, Dave.
DAVE	Oh yeah?
CHRIS	I think Tony's got his eye in there.
DAVE	Well I've got enough to deal with.
CHRIS	Bev's taking advantage of the holiday, is she?
DAVE	Not much.
CHRIS	I know. I heard you. Ali was asleep.
DAVE	You never. Shit.
CHRIS	We're in the next room.

DAVE	Shit. Oh no . . . bad news . . .
CHRIS	Sounded interesting. What were you, a spaceman?
DAVE	Sorry, mate . . . Oh what . . .
CHRIS	No need to apologise. It took me back.
DAVE	Oh don't give me that. Ali's great. I mean not my type, but you know?
CHRIS	Yeah, I know what you're saying, Dave.
DAVE	Shall we get going then?
CHRIS	Yeah, suppose so.

(*They begin to move, then* CHRIS *stops.* DAVE *looks at him.*)

DAVE	Are you okay?
CHRIS	Yeah.
DAVE	Oh right . . . come on mate . . . I'll race you.
CHRIS	Actually Dave, I'm not alright.
DAVE	. . . What is it? Snowplough?
CHRIS	No . . . it's nothing to do with this.
DAVE	Oh, right.
CHRIS	Dave, can I tell you something . . . ?
DAVE	What, it's not personal, is it?
CHRIS	I mean I hardly know you . . .
DAVE	I'm the worst person to ask for advice, Chris.
CHRIS	. . . but I've got to tell someone.
DAVE	What is it?
CHRIS	Al doesn't know. But . . . there's a woman at work. I don't love her, but oh, man . . .
DAVE	Good, is it?
CHRIS	Good? She makes me feel like a little kid. She works in the office. I hate being away.

DAVE   Oh yeah?

CHRIS   I mean she is all woman, you know what I mean?

DAVE   I'm getting the picture. How long . . .

CHRIS   Three years. On and off.

DAVE   Three years. A long time.

CHRIS   That's right. I don't love her.

DAVE   So you've said.

CHRIS   But I don't love Al any more, Dave. And this woman, this woman makes me feel, Dave.

DAVE   Oh yeah?

CHRIS   I mean I wish I could tell Al, Dave, but it would kill her. She worships me. And I don't want to leave her.

DAVE   Yeah?

CHRIS   I mean how can you tell the woman you have known for ten years and lived with for seven that sex with someone else is better than sex with her has ever been?

DAVE   It's a difficult one. You could lie.

CHRIS   It's just more . . . urghhh, you know?

DAVE   Yeah?

CHRIS   More . . . sweaty, scratchy . . .

DAVE   Dirty?

CHRIS   Isn't it pathetic?

DAVE   Sounds great to me.

CHRIS   I'm thirty three this week and I feel like a thirteen year old where women are concerned.

DAVE   You could leave Al.

CHRIS   No. She does everything for me.

DAVE   Sounds like you're knackered, mate.

CHRIS   Well thanks.

DAVE	You've got to let one go.
CHRIS	I can't remember the last time me and Al had sex, Dave . . . (*He has a moment, reflects.*)
DAVE	Yeah?
CHRIS	Sorry Dave. I er . . . well I just wanted to get it out, you know, I've kept that in my head for three years. For God's sake don't tell anyone right, no one, or I am knackered - not even Bev.
DAVE	Come on, what do you think I am? What you going to do, Chris?
CHRIS	I don't know.
DAVE	Yeah. (*Musing.*) Difficult one.
CHRIS	(*musing*) Yeah.
DAVE	How old is she?
CHRIS	Twenty eight. Isn't it bloody pathetic? Men and women, all the games, all the attractions. You net one and then you fancy another. The lies, the fantasies, the jealousy.
DAVE	The sex.
CHRIS	Yeah. Men and women? Isn't it a bloody mess, Dave?
DAVE	It is.

(*A beat.*)

But I love it.

BEV	(*offstage*) Dave!

(DAVE *begins to chuckle like a child, and as he does* CHRIS *joins in. The two of them are like schoolboys.*)

CHRIS	Not a word, right?
DAVE	Right.

(*They exit, as the lights fade.*)

Scene Four

The lights rise to reveal a large wooden sauna room. It has two levels, a wooden floor and seats around the back and sides. A red glow comes from the fire, a small bucket and handle are near the fire. Slight steam (for effect) fills the stage. It is quite dimly lit. MELISSA is sat sideways on the top level. She is wearing bikini bottoms, but she is topless. She has a towel draped over her legs and nether regions. Sat beneath her and boiling to death is BEV, who is wearing a full bathing suit. Across from BEV is ALI who is also wearing a full bathing suit. BEV and ALI have towels. It is so warm hardly anyone can speak.

MEL   (*moans*) Hmmmmmmm . . .

ALI   Hmmmmm . . .

MEL   (*moans*) Ooohhhhh . . .

ALI   Mmmmmm . . .

MEL   (*moans*) Ooohhhhh . . . wonderful.

BEV   Warm, isn't it?

ALI   Mmmmm.

BEV   It's burning my nostrils.

ALI   Mmmmm.

MEL   Alison, would you mind putting a little more water on?

ALI   (*reluctantly*) No, no . . .

MEL   Thanks. I want to try and lose some weight.

      (ALI *pours more water on the fire. A burst of steam.*)

ALI   I don't know why Mel, you look great. I wish I looked like that.

MEL   Still a few more pounds to go. Aren't you two warm?

BEV   No . . . No I'm fine.

MEL   You should relax, let your skin breathe. It's good for you.

BEV   I'm getting out in a minute anyway.

ALI   Maybe I'll take my top down when I've got used to it.

MEL	Where are the guys?
BEV	Dave's still skiing. He's got the bug I think.
MEL	Where did you meet him?
ALI	I don't know where Chris is.
BEV	We met at a disco. There was a car promotion thing and he was there.
ALI	He's sweet. You seem suited.
BEV	Before I met him, I was seeing Jason . . .
MEL	Jason?
BEV	Yes he was nice, but he had a problem with his chest. He could only come out in the warm weather so I hardly ever saw him.
MEL	Strictly a summer romance!
BEV	And then there was this bloke I'd met in Greece.
MEL	I adore Greek men.
BEV	Oh yes. He was nice. But he was Greek. It didn't last. I couldn't understand him, and he was very ugly. He had these pits in his face.
ALI	Like an Eccles cake!
BEV	(*laughing*) Oh you know him?
	(*The three of them laugh together.*)
BEV	This is my longest relationship.
MEL	Really, how long?
BEV	Six months.
ALI	A mere blink, Bev.
BEV	Yeah I know, but . . . well you know . . .
MEL	I've been married for three years. And it was wonderful to begin with and now . . . Oooooohhh.
ALI	What's that supposed to mean?

MEL   Now I think relationships should be run by the
             County Council, like the libraries. When you're
             bored with one man you can take him back and
             change him, and on a weekend you can have two
             men out if you promise to have them back first thing
             on Monday.

ALI   And if you got a really good one you could have him
             out on extended loan.

MEL   Chance would be a fine thing.

BEV   But Dave is really funny.

ALI   Chris was funny once . . .

BEV   But I get a bit jealous if he looks at someone else,
             don't you?

ALI   Chris looks at everyone he meets. He looks in the
             mirror and he sees Richard Gere.

MEL   Lucky for you.

ALI   I look at him sometimes, and I see Richard the Third.

BEV   Oh he seems really nice. I can't think of anything to
             say to him, you know, with him being famous.

MEL   Am I missing something?

ALI   He isn't. He does TV voice-overs.

BEV   Oh he is, though.

ALI   Don't say anything to him Bev, he'll think you're
             deep.

BEV   Anyway. I think I'm about done. I said I'd wait in the
             room for Dave to come back. I think Kevin wants to
             play. Do you have characters? We've got Kevin the
             orphan boy, Gringo the Mexican and Bonker the
             mad space creature lost on earth . . . See you later,
             bye . . .

             (BEV *exits. Silence.*)

MEL   Ohhhh, Bonker the space creature. Lost on earth.

ALI   Yeah.

MEL   Sounds interesting. Beam me up Bonker.

ALI	Yeah, maybe Dave's an alien.
MEL	Well he certainly behaves like one.
ALI	Now, now . . . (*Don't be awful.*)
MEL	Do you want some more water on?
ALI	No I'm frying, thanks.
MEL	Don't you find it relaxing?
ALI	Not really. It's burning a hole in my bum.
MEL	Sit on your towel.
ALI	I am. You know we came away for a relaxing break and I've never worked so hard in my life.
MEL	Do you go away often?
ALI	Twice a year, maybe. And a couple of weekend breaks. Chris works a lot of weekends. In fact Chris works a lot. This holiday is . . . a sort of a test I suppose, really.
MEL	A test of what?
ALI	Nerves I think.
MEL	How long have you been married?
ALI	I'm not.
MEL	Oh, I thought . . .
ALI	Everyone does . . . it's just easier than explaining the real situation.
MEL	Oh, sorry.
ALI	It's no big deal, I'm getting used to it now. After ten years of togetherness.
MEL	Why don't you get married?
ALI	That's the sixty four thousand dollar question. I've asked him a hundred times. Begged him, prayed that he might ask me. I had this idea that he would take me away for my birthday and we'd get married in Gambia or somewhere. He keeps promising. "Next year" he says, "next year" . . . but next year is like tomorrow, it never comes. So I don't bother asking

him any more, we live day to day. Three years ago it
looked like it was all on, and then suddenly it was all
off.

MEL   Well at least you're together? That's something.

ALI   Is it?

MEL   Well, isn't it?

ALI   I'm thirty five years old and I'm his girlfriend.
          Sometimes that really gets to me.

MEL   Oh yes - kids.

ALI   Well that's the other thing.

MEL   Can you?

ALI   I think so.

MEL   Can Chris?

ALI   Dunno. He used to try every night.

MEL   Does he want children?

ALI   I don't know what he wants. It's so difficult to talk to
          him seriously.

MEL   I don't suppose it's any consolation but I do know
          what you're talking about. My life isn't all saunas and
          sunbeds.

ALI   No, I'm sure.

MEL   I used to think that life would get easier to
          understand as I got older. I was wrong.

ALI   Not half.

MEL   It makes me dread the future. I don't think I'll be
          able to understand it. It gets so complicated.

ALI   I don't understand Chris. I thought I did.
          Sometimes he's fine and others . . . Do you know
          what the sad thing is? I can't make him want me . . .

MEL   Oh yes you can . . .

ALI   No.
MEL   You could make him want you, if you wanted to.

ALI	I think it's gone too far. Anyway we're alright most of the time. It's just that I have to tell myself that I will never have what I want. And once I've done that, I live in the compromise.
MEL	Sounds awful.
ALI	Oh it's not as grim as it sounds. It has it's high points. And whatever happens I don't want to hurt him.

(*Suddenly the door of the sauna is opened and a stunningly muscular* TONY, *tanned and wearing only a pure white towel enters. A burst of steam. He has just finished working out.*)

TONY	So, my two favourite skiers.
ALI	Hiya.
TONY	Where are the boy racers?
ALI	Chris is probably making a snowman. He's very creative.
TONY	Chris, too much in the head and not enough in the body.
MEL	And what about you Tony, are you too much in the body and not enough in the head?
TONY	Ah, you have another little joke. But I have degree, so I have both. You need more water?
ALI	No . . .
MEL	Yes . . . please.

(TONY *puts more water on the fire, causing steam. During this time he whips off his towel and we see his pale white arse. He sits, with his towel over himself, contented.*)

TONY	That is better, the hotter the better yes. Alison are you not hot? Yes?
ALI	No, no . . . (*Looking.*) Yes I'm warm. But I'm okay.
TONY	It is very warm I think?
ALI	No I'm fine.
TONY	You must breathe, yes.

ALI	Breathe, yes.
TONY	All the skin must breathe.
ALI	No I couldn't, honestly.
TONY	It is okay.
ALI	No, I'm fine, honestly. I'm going soon. By the time I take it off, I'll have to put it back on anyway. (TONY *shrugs*.) Oh, what the hell . . . (*She takes down her bathing costume.*)
TONY	(*reclining*) A good day. Nice English people. Very good.
ALI	(*she is now topless, and shy*) Ahhh. That's it. Feels better. Oh. Well, that's that . . . Good weather, isn't it? So far? Great weather.
TONY	Good weather so far.
ALI	Yes, yes . . . Yes, good weather.
MEL	What do you do when there's no snow, Tony?
TONY	I teach the golf. In summer the tennis, you should see me, very good. And training with the weights. Keeps fit. I work out three times a week in the winter. Yes.
ALI	(*looking at him*) Yes.
TONY	You like? (*His body.*)
ALI	Well . . .
TONY	Is good body, yes? Hard, yes . . .
ALI	Well yes, I mean . . . good, very.
TONY	I like my body. Very important. Good body, good mind, eh?
ALI	John Locke.
TONY	Very good, yes. I train very hard. But the English they come to Europe they want to ski. But they are not so fit.
ALI	No.
TONY	Sometimes not so quiet.

(*The door is opened.* CHRIS *enters. Steam. He is wearing a towel and slip-on shoes. He doesn't see* ALI *or* TONY, *but he does see* MELISSA. *It is far too hot for him, all at sea in the sauna.*)

CHRIS   Aahhh, hell fire . . . hot in here, isn't it? Hot, blimey? Hot. Good grief, burn your skin off. Hiya Melissa, all right, well mmmmm, don't fancy a massage, do you? Hot isn't it?

ALI   Hi, Chris.

CHRIS   (*turning to* ALI) Hi . . . what are you doing?

ALI   Having a sauna.

CHRIS   I mean . . . (*Agog at her topless.*) I mean come on?

TONY   (*from nowhere*) So we are all in the sauna. Yes?

CHRIS   (*turns and sees* TONY) What the . . . bloody hell?

TONY   You have been in the gym, yes?

CHRIS   (*to* ALI) What are you playing at?

TONY   I have been in the gym for two hours, Chris.

MEL   Have you been working out, Chris?

CHRIS   Eh? No . . . no.

ALI   Take your towel off.

CHRIS   I've been playing table football.

MEL   Did you get a sweat on?

CHRIS   I beat a family from Manchester six-three.

ALI   Take your towel off and relax.

CHRIS   What's going on?

ALI   Nothing.

CHRIS   Oh yeah?

ALI   Take your towel off.

CHRIS   No, I'm okay.

ALI   We're abroad. When in Rome . . .

CHRIS   We're not in Rome.

ALI   . . . take it off.

CHRIS   Alright, alright. I was going to anyway. God it's hot.

               (CHRIS *takes off his towel, to reveal some*
               appalling trunks. He sits near ALI, *gives her a very*
               cold glance, sweats and looks at TONY.)

TONY   So here we all are . . .

CHRIS   Yes, not much. (*He can't help but look.*)

TONY   Good times I think.

ALI   Don't you feel relaxed now?

CHRIS   (*fidgeting*) I would if I could breathe.

ALI   Don't look at me like that.

CHRIS   God it's hot. (*He can't settle down at all.*)

TONY   You like hot?

CHRIS   This can't be good for you.

TONY   Is very good.

CHRIS   (*sitting on his hands*) I'm melting.

ALI   Sit still. You get used to it.

CHRIS   Absurd isn't it. Just sat in a box sweating? No one
               knows where to look. Hot isn't it? Let's cool it down a
               bit. (*He throws a bucket of water over the coals.*
               Steam everywhere.)

TONY   So Chris, are we fit for tomorrow?

CHRIS   Yeah.

TONY   You are strong, yes?

ALI   He's quite strong, aren't you?

CHRIS   I'm not bad.

TONY   Good. Good, when we go up the mountain we need
               to be strong in the legs.

CHRIS   I played rugby . . .

ALI	Years ago . . .
TONY	Your legs must be strong for skiing. You have thin legs, Chris. Like a chicken, I think.
CHRIS	They're strong enough, Tony.
TONY	I think Chris here are two women who enjoy the skiing. In the face very good. Full of life. Two very pretty women, don't you think Chris?
CHRIS	Well . . .
MEL	Now we know Al. I think we're being picked up.
ALI	Are all the instructors like you?
TONY	No. I am the best. I enjoy meeting different people and speaking English.
MEL	And breaking a few hearts, eh Tony?
CHRIS	It's warm, isn't it?
TONY	A few.
MEL	Only a few, come on Tony, you can do better than that.
CHRIS	Warm isn't it?
ALI	What did you expect?
CHRIS	It's warm. I might have to go.
ALI	We know. Don't be a baby. Sit still.
TONY	Too warm, Chris? Have a cold shower, then come back. You will feel better I think.
CHRIS	It's too warm for me. I might go to the room.
ALI	Well go out then.
CHRIS	It's too warm.
ALI	Well go out. Have a shower, like Tony says.
CHRIS	It's too warm. I feel like a chicken.
ALI	Well don't sit there, go out.
CHRIS	I'm going out then.
ALI	Well go on then.

CHRIS	Are you coming? We could have a coffee.
ALI	Why?
CHRIS	Aren't you warm?
ALI	I'm okay.
CHRIS	What, so you're saying you're not warm?
ALI	I am warm.
CHRIS	I'm surprised you've still got any clothes on.
ALI	Don't be stupid.
CHRIS	We are English, you know? Have a bit of pride.
ALI	I'm not doing anything wrong.
CHRIS	I can't stand it in here.
ALI	Don't cause a scene.
CHRIS	I'm not. It's just everywhere I go on this holiday I get nothing but ridicule.
ALI	You won at table football.
CHRIS	Big deal.
ALI	I love the way you look.
CHRIS	Oh yeah, well that make's me feel great.
ALI	It should matter. You look lovely, Chris.
TONY	A little underweight maybe.
CHRIS	God its warm.
ALI	Go out then.
CHRIS	I'm sweating like a pig.
ALI	That's the idea.
CHRIS	Let's go Al. I'm too warm, aren't you?
ALI	I'm warm but I'm not going just yet.
CHRIS	Why?
ALI	I don't want to.

CHRIS	So what are you going to do?
ALI	I'm going to sit here.
CHRIS	What, in this heat?
ALI	Yes.
CHRIS	Right. Right, you stay here with the nudists.
ALI	Right. You go.
CHRIS	I am. I can't stand it. My body's not made for it.
ALI	And take your towel.
CHRIS	Don't worry. It's too bloody warm, it's insane . . . see you later . . .

(CHRIS *is now frying. He hurriedly departs. Silence.* ALISON *sits.*)

ALI	I'd better go.
MEL	It is quite warm.
ALI	I'll see you later.
TONY	You go, yes, Chris is not used to the heat. He will be okay, just the heat, sometimes it makes people go like crazy. He will be okay. Don't worry.

(TONY *is exceptionally kind.*)

| ALI | Chris is already crazy, Tony. He was the voice of a Ribena berry. |

(ALISON *casually exits, taking her towel with her. Silence.*)

TONY	You ski good today.
MEL	Don't you ever get tired of the act?
TONY	It is my life. I enjoy.
MEL	But there must be more than skiing?
TONY	Of course. The girls.
MEL	Ah, yes.

TONY The girls think I am so sexy, what can I do? They are always saying, "Tony I have pains in my legs", "my boots pinch a little". I hold them, I enjoy this. And I show off. So I am good so I can show off, they are showing off with their expensive ski suits. They cannot even ski. They are sad. And at the disco, they are so easy. And I am so good at dancing. I am like Patrick Swayze, I think.

MEL You're completely unbelievable.

TONY Not unbelievable. It is the truth.

MEL I bet you slay them in their chalets, eh Tony?

TONY Of course. It is what they want. So they can talk of such a good time back home.

MEL Don't you do all that thigh-slapping stuff?

TONY Ah no . . . not cool. But tomorrow on the mountain they will be there. The men who do the Tyrolean dancing. And we will have fondue, and good beer and a good time. We go up the mountain, half a mile in the chair lift. And maybe tomorrow Chris and Alison will be friends again?

MEL Yes, maybe.

TONY And maybe tomorrow you will let me show you some disco dancing, and we can have a good time?

MEL Well, you never know.

TONY Of course, it is what I say all my life. "Tony, with the English, you never know."

(TONY *stands and pours more water into the fire. A cloud of steam, and the lights dim.*)

Scene Five

A two person chair lift is flown onto the stage. We should get the impression that CHRIS *and* ALI *are in the chair in front of* BEV *and* DAVE *and that* MEL *and* TONY *are in the chair in front of* CHRIS *and* ALISON. *These are played through the "fourth wall" and only referred to. As a very clear evening draws in the sun begins to set, the mist of the mountains rolls down, maybe with a slight smoke effect. A petrified* BEV *and a cool* DAVE *are flown onto the stage.*

BEV   (*calls to* ALI/*audience, takes out a camera*) Ali . . .
               Ali . . . Alison, Chris! Youooooo! Want a photo?
               Smile. Come on put your arms around her . . . come
               on, Chris . . .

DAVE   He daren't move.

BEV   Smile. Say "cheese".

DAVE   (*shouts*) Say Cheddar, Chris. Might come in handy in
               the future.

BEV   (*takes the picture*) Gotcha . . . Great thanks, you take
               one of us too when we get to the top . . .

DAVE   Have you finished?

BEV   Yeah.

DAVE   Well give us that camera David Bailey, before you
               drop it.

BEV   (*handing over the camera*) Oh, I like it when you
               look after me Dave.

DAVE   Oh, yeah . . .

BEV   Have we stopped Dave?

DAVE   Yeah.

BEV   Oh, I don't like it.

DAVE   Somebody's probably fallen off at the bottom.

BEV   (*becoming more concerned*) Oh, I don't like it babe.

DAVE   Just sit still, we'll be away in a minute.

BEV   But I don't like it.

DAVE   I've heard you.

BEV   I don't though.

DAVE   (*losing patience*) Look, sit still and shut up.

BEV   But I don't like it . . .

DAVE   Well there's not much we can do about it is there,
               we're five miles in the air stuck in a bleeding chair
               lift.

BEV   Is that how high we are?

DAVE   Oh God . . .

             (*Silence.*)

BEV   Have you got a mood on, babe?

DAVE   No.

BEV   You look like you have.

DAVE   Well I haven't, okay.

BEV   (*satisfied*) Oh. (*Silence. Then, to* ALI.) We're stuck. Yeah. Good fun isn't it? Yeah, brilliant. Look babe, Tony's got his arm around Melissa.

DAVE   Oh yeah?

BEV   (*noticing* CHRIS) I don't think Chris likes being stuck, babe.

DAVE   You and him should team up Bev. You make a pair.

             (*Pause.*)

BEV   Are these things safe, babe?

DAVE   Yeah.

BEV   (*looks above her head at the cable*) I don't think that wire's very safe, do you?

DAVE   (*joking*) No, you're right.

BEV   Are you sure they're safe?

DAVE   Apparently last year about this time, one of those wires snapped and everyone plunged to their deaths.

BEV   Oh you're joking?

DAVE   No I'm not, its true.

             (DAVE *rocks the chair.*)

BEV   Don't babe, don't! (*He stops.* BEV *is now distracted by looking outside the chair lift beneath her.*) Look at all the houses, Dave, aren't they small?

DAVE   Well, we are five miles in the sky.

BEV   Which is our hotel, Dave?

DAVE   That one with the snow on it.

           (BEV *looks beneath her at all the thousands of
           hotels.*)

BEV   They've all got snow on them, Dave.

DAVE   I know Bev, I was being amusing.

BEV   Oh, I didn't realise . . .

DAVE   (*playing*) Now don't you go all moody boody? Come
           here, don't worry about this lift Bev, it goes up here
           a hundred times a day.

           (DAVE *puts his arm around her for comfort.*)

BEV   Yeah but not with me in it.

DAVE   (*looks between his legs*) Look that's our hotel Bev,
           near the railway station.

BEV   (*looking down*) Oh yeah babe, aren't you clever?

DAVE   Yeah.

BEV   (*sees something, shocked*) Oh look at that, a Moose!

DAVE   (*looks*) That's not a Moose . . . it's a hoose . . .

BEV   Don't be stupid, Dave.

DAVE   It wasn't me, it was Kevin.

BEV   Where is he anyway?

DAVE   Dunno.

BEV   I haven't seen him since this morning.

           (DAVE *suddenly sees Kevin beneath them.*)

DAVE   Look Bev, Kevin's down there!

BEV   Where? (*She looks.*)

DAVE   Down there. Look. "Hiya Kevin! All right mate?"

BEV   I can't see him, babe.

DAVE   He's there. Look Bev, in that sauna with those two
           Swedish nymphos.

BEV   (*giving up*) Oh don't babe. (*Pause.*) What were you
          talking to Melissa about, babe?

DAVE   When?

BEV   In the hotel before we came out?

DAVE   Nothing.

BEV   Oh.

DAVE   Just having a chat.

BEV   You just seemed to be having a laugh with her, that's
          all.

DAVE   Well I can have a laugh, can't I?

BEV   'Course you can.

DAVE   Good.

BEV   You just seemed to be very cosy, that's all.

DAVE   Well I was trying to tell her a joke.

BEV   Oh.

DAVE   Then you turned up.

BEV   What sort of joke was it, babe?

DAVE   It would have been a funny joke Bev, but you
          ruined it.

BEV   Oh sorry. Was it a dirty joke?

DAVE   No.

BEV   I'll bet it was?

DAVE   Alright, it was.

BEV   Good job I came over then, babe. Anyway I was
          looking for Kevin.

DAVE   (*saddened*) Exactly.

BEV   What?

DAVE   And could you not call me Kevin in front of the
          whole hotel?

BEV	Well . . .
DAVE	It is just a little bit too much Bev, you know?
BEV	Don't you like Kevin?
DAVE	'Course I do. But that's just something for me and you.
BEV	I just thought it was a way of showing the world our affection, babe.
DAVE	(*dead*) Well, it's not.
BEV	Sorry. Babe?
DAVE	Yeah.
BEV	(*light*) Kevin? Kevin?
DAVE	Kevin's not in, Bev. He's out playing.
BEV	He's not.
DAVE	(*dead*) He is. He's been saying some horrible things about you.
BEV	Has he?
DAVE	He says he hates you.
BEV	He doesn't?
DAVE	He says you're stupid, he says you're embarrassing.
BEV	What's he been saying that for?
DAVE	How should I know?

(*The chair lift begins to move.* BEV *cheers and hugs* DAVE.)

BEV	(*shouting to* ALI) Ali, we're going! Oooooohh!
DAVE	(*shouting to* CHRIS) Hold tight, Chris, we'll soon be there . . .

(DAVE *gives a sarcastic laugh, and squeezes* BEV. *She screams, and in a flourish of excitement, the chair is flown off into the wings.* Abba's "Money, Money, Money" *plays and the lights change.*)

Scene Six

A mountain top. Many ferns, a small wooden seat, worn by the weather. The moon is out and the clear dark blue sky glitters with stars, all of them incredibly bright. As the music fades, the lights reveal CHRIS *and* ALI. *Things are very tetchy between them.* CHRIS *is downstage, looking at the world.*

ALI   Top of the world. Doesn't it make you feel small?

CHRIS It does . . .

ALI   Amazing, look at the sky. Isn't it big?

CHRIS What did you expect?

ALI   Oh you're never romantic with me.

CHRIS I am, I am. You don't recognise it. I just have a funny way of showing it.

ALI   No you're never romantic the way I want you to be.

CHRIS Don't start it please.

ALI   How high above sea level are we, do you know?

CHRIS No idea.

ALI   A thousand feet?

CHRIS I've really no idea. Five thousand, I don't know.

ALI   Oh right, playing that game are we?

CHRIS No I'm not playing any game. Not with you anyway.

ALI   Oh Chris. Why is everything I do a problem for you?

CHRIS You're the only problem.

ALI   Please!

CHRIS You love it don't you, because you can ski and I can't?

ALI   What?

CHRIS You love it.

ALI   I can't help it if you can't ski. You're doing alright. Who gives a fig anyway?

CHRIS	I do. I do.
ALI	Can we leave it Chris, those people are waiting for us.
CHRIS	Why can't we be on our own anyway?
ALI	They're nice people, that's what you do when you go on holiday. You meet other people.
CHRIS	I don't.
ALI	No, you don't.
CHRIS	(*hard*) This relationship is over.
ALI	Don't give me the boredom routine.
CHRIS	You bore me.
ALI	Oh do I? So what else is new?
CHRIS	Yes you do.
ALI	And you don't bore me?
CHRIS	I'm a highly sexed person, you aren't.
ALI	(*still, angry*) Thank you. Thank you. Thank you for that, that's just what I want to hear.
CHRIS	Do you want to know something?
ALI	Go on try and hurt me some more why don't you?
CHRIS	I don't find you attractive any more.
ALI	(*knowing*) Oh wow, well thanks for that as well.
CHRIS	You forced me to say it.
ALI	Do you think I don't know that? Do you think I haven't actually noticed? You must be blind, you're so self-centred you can't see beyond you're nose. I can't even remember the last time you were nice to me. I can't even remember the last time you touched me, except to say shift your fat arse. Do you think that's being loving, eh?
CHRIS	I'm not bothered about you any more.
ALI	You'd be bothered if I left you.
CHRIS	Well that's where you're wrong.

ALI	You'd be bothered if I went off with someone.
CHRIS	I wouldn't.
ALI	If I went off it would kill you.
CHRIS	I could cope without you.
ALI	Oh yeah. You don't know what day it is half the time.
CHRIS	You couldn't cope if I went off with someone.
ALI	No one would have you, believe me.
CHRIS	Oh really?
ALI	They'd have to be Jesus Christ to put up with you. No one wants you except me, Chris.
CHRIS	Well that's where you're wrong.
ALI	Oh really?
CHRIS	Yes.
ALI	Well it wouldn't surprise me if you'd been seeing somebody behind my back. Who is it, is it Val or June or Cathy, which one of those slags have you been seeing at work? I wouldn't put it past you. (ALI *begins to boil*.)
CHRIS	Well you're wrong again aren't you?
ALI	Am I?
CHRIS	Yes.
ALI	Am I?
CHRIS	Yes.
ALI	Am I?
CHRIS	Yes.
ALI	Really?
CHRIS	Yes.
ALI	Tell the truth.
CHRIS	I am.
ALI	Tell the truth.

CHRIS	I am.
ALI	(*shouting*) Tell me the truth, Chris!
CHRIS	I am.
ALI	Tell me the truth, Chris.
CHRIS	You're crazy . . .
ALI	Tell me the truth.
CHRIS	(*shouting*) I'm telling you. I'm telling you the truth.
ALI	Are you?
CHRIS	Yes, yes, yes! How many more times?

(*Both are very angry and upset, breathing hard and heavy.*)

I'm telling you the truth, Alison.

(*Silence.*)

ALI	No, you're not.

(*A sudden gush of energy.* BEV, MELISSA, DAVE *and* TONY *enter. They are togged up for an evening in the Alps.*)

BEV	Hiya . . . isn't it amazing?
DAVE	Where's the oxygen? Arrhhh! (*He mimes suffocating.*)
TONY	Here you are, very good. Having a romantic time? You like?
ALI	It's brilliant.
TONY	Okay so now we can all go and let the good times roll?
BEV	Let's just have a photo shall we, a photo of everyone on the mountain, come on, all together.

(BEV *has a small automatic camera. The group assemble,* DAVE *near* MELISSA, TONY *near* ALI, CHRIS *waits for* BEV. *The camera is on the floor so they have to make daft shapes to be in the shot.* BEV *rushes forward, and grabs* CHRIS.)

BEV   Smile everyone . . .

ALL   Arrhhhhhh!

              (*They all cheer, the camera flashes, a lightbulb
              effect.*)

TONY   And now we must go. And as we go we will sing
              famous Austrian song. It is important in the mountain
              to sing the correct song. It is a song you may not
              know. Okay. (*Sings.*) Here ve go, here ve go, here
              ve go . . .

              (*They all join in, jostling, embracing and having an
              excellent time. They sing one verse and stop, all
              laugh.*)

              Very good, you learn so quick, you are my best
              school ever. Yes?

ALL   (*a cheer*) Yes!

              (*Another euphoric cheer. They freeze. Abba plays.
              Blackout.*)

              End of Act One

ACT TWO

Scene One

*Night. We are on the snowy area just outside the hotel. A number
of trees. Skis are stuck into the snow. The stars twinkle in the
heavens. It is about four in the morning, a full day later. On stage,
down left is a small snowman with a scarf and hat. The peace of
the night is shattered when* DAVE *and* BEV *arrive from upstage on
a sledge, and speed downstage to the snowman. They are
laughing and cheering, having just had a great night. They've had
a little too much to drink, and are singing as the sledge comes down.*

DAVE "The hills are alive with the sound of music!"

(The sledge stops. Both fall off.)

BEV (*sings*) "High on a hill lived a lonely
goatherd . . . yodelee, yodelee, ooooow!"

*(They make great play from their drunken yodelling,
and as they do,* CHRIS *enters with a carrot for the
snowman. He places the carrot in the snowman's face.
It is now complete.* CHRIS *too, has had a drink.)*

What's he doing? What are you doing, Chris?

CHRIS It's a snowman.

DAVE Chris . . . it's four in the morning.

CHRIS Cue for a song. I thought you'd be back earlier.

BEV You missed a great night Chris, wasn't it babe, Kev,
er, Dave, great wasn't it? Even better than last night,
the fondue thingy.

DAVE Great night, Schnaps a-go-go.

CHRIS It's for Al, we had a bit of a tiff.

BEV Is that why you didn't come Chris?

CHRIS You know what its like, it's all show. We love each
other like mad, we just don't show it.

DAVE Keep it a secret, eh?

CHRIS Is she coming?

BEV   Oh that's nice, isn't that nice babe, Kev, what a nice
               thought, he's made Al a snowman. Isn't that romantic.
               Chris, she won't be able to take it home you know?

DAVE   Hasn't got a ticket anyway, Bev.

BEV   Oh, I want a snowman.

DAVE   I'll make you one when we get in.

BEV   Won't it melt?

DAVE   I'll make it in the fridge.

BEV   I want a snowman.

DAVE   (*to* CHRIS) You've set her off now. (*Back to* BEV.)
               Come on you, let's have you in bed . . .

BEV   No.

DAVE   Yes, you've made a fool of yourself quite enough for
               one night.

BEV   I haven't.

DAVE   She said she could speak German, Chris. She went to
               the bar for a couple of drinks, fifty minutes later she
               was still there, a crowd had gathered around her,
               they thought she was a mime artist. (*To* BEV, *mocking
               but meaning it.*) You're stupid aren't you, eh Bev,
               stupid?

BEV   I was trying to mime it.

DAVE   Come on you lets have you. I want you in bed with
               your sexiest gear on.

BEV   I've only got my thermals.

DAVE   They'll do . . . come on. Come on, race you . . .

               (DAVE *sets off to race,* BEV *is off and exits quickly.*
               DAVE *watches her go and looks at* CHRIS.)

               Stupid bitch.

CHRIS   Is Al coming, Dave?

DAVE   On her way, I think. She was putting 'em away,
               steaming when we left. She's probably come the short

cut. Bev wanted to sledge down the mountain. Stupid bitch. Hey Chris, I bet you fifty quid I beat you in the slalom.

CHRIS No I'm not a betting man, Dave.

DAVE Come on . . .

CHRIS Tell you what - I'll bet Kevin fifty pence.

DAVE Fifty pence, you're on. When I see Kev I'll tell him.

(DAVE *drifts towards the hotel entrance and exits from the stage.* CHRIS *attends to the snowman. He straightens his scarf.*)

CHRIS Come on smile . . . it's not that cold, is it? Where's your Mum, eh? Where is she, she's a dirty stop out isn't she? Eh?

(*As* CHRIS *speaks to the snowman,* ALI, *drunk but fighting against it, appears from the same entrance upstage that* BEV *and* DAVE *appeared from.* CHRIS *looks at her, silence between them, but the dialogue is caring.*)

Late aren't you?

ALI I thought you weren't talking. I thought you weren't bothered about me?

CHRIS I say some stupid things, you know that.

ALI What's that?

CHRIS What's it look like?

ALI Two snowmen.

CHRIS You're not that drunk are you?

ALI Dunno.

CHRIS I built it for you.

ALI Why?

CHRIS It's a monument to our relationship.

ALI A snowman's about right.

CHRIS	It's a peace offering. I'm calling a truce, no arguing on hols, remember?
ALI	After all you've said?
CHRIS	I say stupid things.
ALI	Yeah.
CHRIS	I thought I was being romantic.
ALI	(*looking at the snowman*) Is it supposed to be you?
CHRIS	No.
ALI	It looks a bit like my Dad.
CHRIS	No, its just a snowman.
ALI	The head's deformed.
CHRIS	It's just a snowman, that's all.
ALI	(*trying to focus*) Got a funny nose. . . It is you, it is you, isn't it?
	(*Pause.*)
CHRIS	I missed you.
ALI	You only want me when I'm not here.
CHRIS	That's not true, Al.
ALI	You're never nice to me.
CHRIS	I am.
ALI	No you're not.
CHRIS	I buy you things don't I? That's my way of being romantic.
ALI	You buy me such ridiculous things.
CHRIS	Like what?
ALI	A book on self-defence. A tummy toner.
CHRIS	You've got everything.

ALI You bought me a book about the sinking of the Titanic, as if I'm interested? You only bought it for me so that you could read it. When I was twenty six you bought me a facial sauna. To get rid of my spots you said.

CHRIS You said that was what you wanted!

ALI I'd only had it a week and you wanted to use it.

CHRIS That was a joke.

ALI On my thirtieth birthday you sent me a card. Can you remember?

CHRIS Why drag this up?

ALI It had, "In deepest sympathy" written on it.

CHRIS It actually said, "Thinking of you in your time of grief." I thought it was funny.

ALI It was, funny for you. I'm going to bed.

(*She makes to move.*)

CHRIS Al, I do love you. There is no one else but you. Honest.

ALI I don't know where I am with you any more, Chris. One moment you say you hate me, then you tell me you love me. I don't know where I am any more.

CHRIS Al, this snowman will never melt, and neither will our love!

ALI I'm going to bed Chris, I feel sick.

(ALISON *wanders slowly towards the hotel.* CHRIS *looks on. She exits.*)

CHRIS Well don't vomit on my side.

(CHRIS *looks at the snowman, sombre, quiet.*)

She doesn't like you, does she. You're not deformed, are you?

(*He embraces the snowman. A sombre Abba track plays, the lights dim.*)

Scene Two

The hotel lobby. Day. MEL *approaches the reception area and rings the bell. She looks into the reception, but no one is around.*

MEL   Hello? Hello . . . Hello?

(TONY *enters through another entrance, behind her.*)

TONY   Hallo?

MEL   Hiya.

TONY   Good morning to you, all is well, yes?

MEL   Just about. I was hoping for a message.

TONY   There is nobody there!

MEL   Very true.

TONY   You have a good night last night. Much good times, yes?

MEL   Fantastic thanks. But I think the Gluwien eventually got to me this morning. My head.

TONY   Ah yes the head. Tony he does not drink so he does not get the head. But a great night. We do the same again tonight, I think.

MEL   I don't think I can take the pace.

TONY   Oh yes, you must. You ski today, there is good snow on the Rosschutte. Today I must see the Trish, the rep. Next school only a few days away, already it is time to go home I think. I must check, maybe lots of crazy English, like Keystone Kops I think. I am very busy today. Sometimes I think I work too hard. Very early in the morning and very late in the evening. Work, work, work. I think I work too much, eh, not enough time to play. But I go. You ring the bell, maybe they will come, maybe not. I see you.

(CHRIS *enters.* TONY *sees him.*)

(*as he exits*) Ah, Chris . . . good morning.

CHRIS   Hi, Tony.

(TONY exits. MEL rings the bell once more. No response. As she waits, CHRIS grabs his chance of a chat-up.)

CHRIS   Here she is, the best skier in Seefeld.

MEL   Flattery will get you everywhere this morning.

CHRIS   Are you suffering as well?

MEL   Just between the eyes.

CHRIS   I'll hold you to that race later if you fancy it.

MEL   Do you think you're ready? *(She turns and rings the bell once more.)*

CHRIS   I think so. You could always help me out on the parallel turn.

MEL   When do you fly back?

CHRIS   Wednesday.

MEL   I think I might need a little more time, Chris.

CHRIS   In that case I'll stay here. Great, isn't it? A picture postcard.

MEL   Yes, I love the snow.

CHRIS   You know, I thought that this might be a bit down-market for someone like you.

MEL   Oh really, someone like me?

CHRIS   Well I'd've thought you'd be better off up at Klosters with the rich and famous.

MEL   Spotting Charles and Di?

CHRIS   That sort of thing.

MEL   Well sometimes. But I also like a change. Sometimes, Chris, I like to slum it.

CHRIS   Like a bit of the rough stuff, eh?

MEL   Within reason.

CHRIS	Oh right. I was beginning to think I wasn't even in with a chance.
MEL	A chance of what?
CHRIS	Well . . . I don't often get a chance to talk to chat to other women, Melissa. I lead a very quiet life.
MEL	(*ringing the bell once more*) Oh come on, you're not shy, surely?
CHRIS	In all the time Ali and I have been together I've only spoken to one other woman. I'm very dangerous, you see.
MEL	(*mocking*) Oh yes, I can see that.
CHRIS	(*self mocking*) Yeah, I'm very dangerous. You see, although they don't realise it women find me irresistable.
MEL	Really?
CHRIS	Yes. It happens all the time.
MEL	Chris? Are you joking?
	(*A beat.*)
CHRIS	Yes, yeah I'm sorry, I just get carried away.
MEL	You're ever so funny, Chris.
	(*She means this, but turns and rings the bell. As she does,* BEV *and* DAVE *enter dressed for skiing.*)
DAVE	Morning, all. Hello Melissa. Come on, Chris. Get some practice in. I'm taking your money, mate.
CHRIS	I'm just getting some tips from Mel.
DAVE	Oh yeah, what is it, private tuition?
CHRIS	Don't be jealous, Dave.
BEV	He wants to practice all the time now, he's got the bug. I wanted a lay-in this morning but I couldn't have one - Kevin was up at six.
DAVE	Come on, Bev. (*He exits.*)

BEV	I'm coming. My legs ache, my ankles are killing me . . . you should see my big toe, Chris - it's blue.
CHRIS	At least you're still in one piece.
BEV	Just. See you later.

(BEV *hobbles hopelessly after* DAVE. CHRIS *looks at* MEL, *then after* DAVE *and* BEV.)

CHRIS	The perfect couple. It's their first holiday together.
MEL	And they're making the most of it.
CHRIS	Not half.
MEL	Good for them.
CHRIS	You know, I can't work it out Melissa.
MEL	What?
CHRIS	You.
MEL	There's nothing to work out, is there?
CHRIS	Oh come on, of course there is. You're here on your own, and you're not liking it much.
MEL	Aren't I?
CHRIS	Tell the truth Melissa. I lie for a living, I can see a lie a mile off. Something's not quite right. I don't know what it is, but I'm right, aren't I? Is it Tony? You're not interested in him, are you?
MEL	He's very attractive.
CHRIS	He is, he is, and from what I've seen he's got all the right equipment.
MEL	Mmmm . . . he has but you're a mile out, Chris.
CHRIS	Am I?
MEL	Yes.
CHRIS	Funny, I don't think I am.
MEL	Well you are.

CHRIS   Is it a divorce?

MEL   No, I'm married.

CHRIS   Happily?

MEL   Ish . . .

CHRIS   Ha ha, I knew, got it in two. An unhappy marriage.

MEL   I wouldn't go that far.

CHRIS   Where is he then?

MEL   Away on business. Brussels to be precise.

CHRIS   Away on business. Come on, Melissa, you can do better than that.

MEL   It's the truth. Peter's gone to Brussels. I flew up here to ski. It's all very straightforward. Alison must have some fun with you Chris, your imagination works overtime.

CHRIS   I can just picture him. Tall, slightly older than you, greying maybe? Public school education, maybe Oxbridge, played his fair share of rugger. Terribly, terribly. He has a personal secretary. She's dark, maybe Oriental, travels everywhere with him, they're close, but not too close. He thinks it's strictly business, but she has fantasies.

          (MEL *turns and rings the bell.*)

          But he'll never be unfaithful, and you know that. Even though all the girls in the office think he's great, you know he's only a flirt.

MEL   I think I've heard enough Chris, thanks.

CHRIS   But am I on the right track? Or is he a short fat bald man from Exeter?

MEL   He's somewhere in between.

CHRIS   And what about the personal secretary?

MEL   Yes, he has a secretary, she's very nice. She's not Oriental, she's from Leeds actually. And yes, I suspect Peter's actually thought about doing something. Most men do, don't they?

CHRIS	I think you're very attractive, Melissa.
MEL	I beg your pardon.
CHRIS	I said I think you are very attractive.
MEL	Oh, now . . . look.
CHRIS	Very *very* attractive.
MEL	Please, Chris.
CHRIS	I mean it.
MEL	Look . . .
CHRIS	I do.
MEL	Look, I think you're misreading all this.
CHRIS	I mean it.
MEL	Thank you.
CHRIS	When I saw you in the sauna, I thought you looked fantastic.
MEL	I think I should go, Chris.
CHRIS	I think you're really sexy.
MEL	I think you'd better stop now, Chris. I think you're reading this all wrong.
CHRIS	Am I?
MEL	Yes, you are.
CHRIS	You're really sexy.
MEL	Stop it, Chris!
CHRIS	Yeah, yeah you're right.
MEL	Let's just forget it, yeah?
CHRIS	Yeah, yeah. Let's forget it.
MEL	Fine. Look I must go. See you later? (*She makes to leave.*)
CHRIS	For that race?

MEL	Yeah, yeah, sure.
CHRIS	Mel?

(*She stops, turns.*)

MEL	Yes?
CHRIS	Look. I do really think you are something else.
MEL	I know Chris, you've told me. Now I must really . . .
CHRIS	But I haven't told you really, have I?
MEL	Told me what?
CHRIS	That I'd really like to fuck you!
MEL	Thanks Chris, but I've got to get back to earth.

(MEL *exits to the snow.*)

CHRIS   (*calling after her*) Yeah, Yeah, don't forget about the race . . . (*Turns, to himself.*) You stuck up cow!

(CHRIS *walks downstage, bemoaning his recent performance.*)

My God what am I saying? All sorts of drivel is coming out of my mouth. I've got to learn to control my mouth. I must realise that not every woman in the world wants to have sex with me. Sad but true. She must think that I'm some sort of pervert. Oh, Chris, Chris . . . You need help, mate.

Hello, caller on line four. Hello, Chris, this is Chris. There's this woman and wowwww! - she's fantastic! Melissa, Melissa, I can't get you out of my head. There we are rolling around in the cold snow. Everything is erect and standing to attention. Oh my God what a woman. You are driving me crazy. I can see it all, all in my head, me and you. There we are naked in the snow, you're naked, I'm almost naked. We're rolling around in the snow, flakes falling onto our bodies, and I've got cramp. You look stunning, your lips glossed and shining, the melting snow forming rivulets down your breasts, your hair radiant against the light. You feel like silk, taste like soft, smooth chocolate.

Everything else in the world diminishes, you are mine. We are making love so slowly, so subtly, so amazingly and in the background, very faintly, I hear music. No, not the gentle pulse of Mozart, not the breathtaking swirl of Strauss. It was Abba!

(*Upstage, a massive grand piano is flown in. Abba music plays.* TONY, *dressed as Abba pianist,* BEV *as Abba singer,* ALI *as other singer, in wigs and* DAVE *as singer stand upstage and mime to Abba.*)

CHORUS   Super Trouper, beams are gonna blind me,
          But I won't feel blue,
          Like I always do;
          'Cos somewhere in the crowd there's you.

(*Over the instrumental,* CHRIS *continues.*)

I swear it was Abba. There in the snow, Benny and Bjorn were playing. They were wearing white leggings with gold boob tubes and the video in my head was Super Trouper, my favourite, recorded in 1980.

ALI   (*as Frieda*) I was sick and tired of everything when I called you last night from Glasgow. All I do is eat and sleep and sing. Wishing every show was the last show. Can't imagine I was glad to hear you coming, suddenly I feel alright. And it's gonna be so different when I'm on the stage tonight.

CHORUS   Tonight the Super Trouper lights are gonna find me,
          Shining like the sun,
          Smiling, having fun,
          Feeling like a number one;
          Tonight the Super Trouper beams are gonna find me,
          But I won't feel blue,
          Like I always do,
          'Cos somewhere in the crowd there's you.

CHRIS   The next thing I know I'm skiing. I'm out of the room, Benny and Bjorn have buggered off and I'm skiing on the Thomas lift.

(*The piano is flown out, Abba exit. Lights change, and music plays under.*)

I am actually skiing with confidence down the gentle bumps of the Thomas lift. I start slowly at first, awkward, bent double, and then faster and faster, and faster and the wind whistles past me, and I stand up, and feel the cold, invigorating on my face, pinching my nose, freezing my ears. Faster and faster and in my head Abba still plays, a song from their Greatest Hits Album.

(*A burst of music.* CHRIS *responds heroically.*)

I was passing little kids, I was passing old women. I was actually passing people of my own age. I felt so free, so alive, so successful . . . and for the first time I realised that I was deeply in love with Al. I couldn't believe it. I actually admitted to myself that I loved her. That no one else in the world mattered, that the affair was over and we were in love so deep you couldn't believe it. And for the first time in my life it felt fantastic.

(*Abba music, 'Head Over Heels'.* CHRIS *exits. Lights change. Fantasy is over. Harsh reality returns.*)

Scene Three

High on the slopes. It is a bright morning. We see DAVE *ski down the corner of the slope. He turns at the bottom and calls upstage.*

DAVE Come on . . . come on . . . ohhhh. What are you doing?

(*Silence.*)

Come on, how long are you going to be? It's great, it's a doddle, you did it yesterday. Come on, you stupid bitch, try.

(*Slowly and very frightened,* BEV *shuffles onto the stage. Her bottle has completely gone, and she is petrified.* DAVE *is cruel.*)

Come on.

BEV Don't shout.

DAVE Just try for once.

BEV I am.

DAVE You're not.

BEV I am.

DAVE Come on . . . you stupid cow.

BEV Don't, babe . . .

DAVE   Come on, babe.

(BEV *is desperately stuck.*)

BEV   I can't.

DAVE   Put your skis together and come down.

(BEV *has one ski crossed over the other and her poles in front of her skis.*)

BEV   I can't.

DAVE   You can.

BEV   I can't!

DAVE   You can.

BEV   I can't babe, I can't move!

DAVE   Bev, don't be pathetic. You can.

(*Pause.*)

BEV   I'm stuck.

DAVE   You're not.

BEV   I am.

DAVE   You've just lost confidence that's all. Take a deep breath and schuss down, you've done it before, just turn and schuss down . . . whooosh, come on . . . come on . . . come on, babe . . .

BEV   (*pathetic*) I can't!

DAVE   You're blocking the rest of the hill.

BEV   I know.

DAVE   Well come down then.

BEV   I can't.

DAVE   (*slightly annoyed*) Bev, you are blocking all the hill, now stop messing about and come down the hill.

BEV   (*outraged*) I can't help it, what do you want me to do?

DAVE   I want you to come down!

BEV   Don't shout at me, babe.

DAVE   (*under breath*) What do you want me to do, come up
             and get you? (*Normal.*) Look babe, all you have to
             do is get your weight on your other leg.

BEV   (*shouting*) I daren't move!

DAVE   (*shouting back*) You'll have to move!

BEV   I daren't.

DAVE   You'll have to.

BEV   I'm stuck, you'll have to come and get me.

DAVE   Bev, you're stuck up a hillick, not Everest. You're
             acting childish, just come down.

BEV   I didn't want to come out today.

DAVE   Don't start moaning.

BEV   I said it was too cold for me today, my chest gets
             tight, Dave. I didn't feel like coming out today.

             (BEV *is now close to tears.*)

DAVE   Oh, don't start crying, for pity's sake don't start
             crying, your face'll freeze up. On second thoughts,
             cry Bev, cry . . .

BEV   Babe?

DAVE   Just try Bev, just try.

BEV   I'm trying.

             (*She moves her body about half an inch.*)

DAVE   You're not even moving.

BEV   I'm scared babe. I can't do it.

DAVE   Well I'm not coming up for you, so either you come
             down yourself or you freeze to death.

BEV   Oh babe?

DAVE   No I'm not coming for you.

BEV   Why are you like this Dave? I only came for you. I try and do everything for you. (*She is crying now.*) I can't help it if I can't do it. I'm trying. I'm trying. You haven't got any idea how hard it is for me. I'm not like you, I can't run and do physical things. I just can't. Can you please try and understand?

DAVE   There's no need for tears.

BEV   Try and understand me, babe.

DAVE   I'm still not coming for you Bev.

BEV   I've always been weak at sports Dave, please, please, please, please . . . (*Screaming insanely.*) Please . . . !

DAVE   No.

       (BEV *feigns having a coughing fit, her chest is tight.*)

BEV   Babe . . . oh my chest. (*Coughs.*) Oh babe? Babe? (*Coughs.*) Babe . . .

DAVE   Come on you stupid bitch. Just let yourself come down.

BEV   Babe . . . babe, babe . . .

DAVE   (*shouts*) Come on . . .

       (BEV *turns in her skis and makes a movement forward, but she falls. The fall is innocuous, but the scream that accompanies the fall is blood-curdling.* BEV *hits the deck with a thump.*)

BEV   I did it. (*Through tears.*) Love me, babe, love me, Kevin.

       (*Abba plays, "Knowing Me, Knowing You". Lights change.*)

Scene Four

Evening. A hotel room. A small double bed, lamp and small wardrobe all in pine. As the lights rise, ALISON *is sitting very quietly in a chair, reading. She is subdued and hurt for some reason. She wears a dressing gown.* CHRIS *enters, wearing après ski gear. He is carrying some ferns, which he hides behind his back. He seems almost a different* CHRIS, *genuinely kind.*

CHRIS	Al . . . Ali. Ali. Are you talking to me? Al? I've got you something. Al?
ALI	Yeah?
CHRIS	Feel better now?
ALI	Yeah, a bit.
CHRIS	Good.
ALI	Where've you been?
CHRIS	Thinking, sorting things out.
ALI	Makes a change.
CHRIS	Are you alright now?
ALI	Yes.
CHRIS	I, erm . . . I've bought you these. Ten years you've had to wait for them but here they are.
	(He offers her the ferns.)
ALI	Oh, right. What are they?
CHRIS	I don't know, I just bought them.
ALI	There was no need.
CHRIS	They're not flowers, but it was all they had.
ALI	They're nice.
CHRIS	It's the thought that counts.
ALI	Chris?
CHRIS	What?
ALI	I've got something to tell you.
CHRIS	So have I.
ALI	It's your fault, Chris.
CHRIS	What?
ALI	Last night I did something stupid.
CHRIS	Something stupid . . .

ALI	I was wrong, Chris. I didn't mean to but I did and I can't bear the guilt. I've got to tell you.
CHRIS	What?
ALI	I don't know why I have to I feel like a sixteen year old.
CHRIS	What? Tell me what?
ALI	It just happened.
CHRIS	What?
ALI	Last night.
CHRIS	What? What? What last night, what happened?
ALI	I can't tell you.
CHRIS	Tell me.
ALI	I can't.
CHRIS	What? Tell me what?
ALI	Why do I feel so guilty?
CHRIS	What?
ALI	Stop shouting.
CHRIS	Well just tell me, tell me. What?
ALI	I was drunk.
CHRIS	So was I.
ALI	I had too much to drink, and, one thing led to another . . .
CHRIS	One thing led to another?
ALI	And . . . I slept with Tony.
CHRIS	You . . .
	(*Silence.*)
ALI	I slept with Tony.
	(*The horror takes his breath away.*)
CHRIS	Oh my God. Oh . . . oh . . . no . . . no . . .

ALI   Chris.

CHRIS   Oh my God.

ALI   I did it, and I'm telling you and that's it.

CHRIS   You're joking, tell me you're joking?

ALI   No.

CHRIS   (*staggered as if by a bereavement*) Ohhh . . .
           (*Breathless.*) . . . Ohhhhh.

ALI   I had to tell you.

CHRIS   No you didn't.

ALI   You asked me, you made me. I was drunk. You said
           some awful things to me this week. He's the only
           person who's been nice to me. I'm sorry.

CHRIS   Sorry? Sorry? . . .

ALI   Okay. Kill me, hit me . . . I didn't do it to hurt you. I
           thought you meant what you said last night?

CHRIS   I say a lot of things. Why did you come back? Why
           didn't you stay, you could have at least done him the
           honour of staying. Or was there a queue?

ALI   I came back because I love you so much.

CHRIS   Rubbish. I don't believe this, this is just a nightmare.
           I'm sat listening to the radio and you are in bed with
           one of the Von Trapps?

ALI   It wasn't anything.

CHRIS   I knew as soon as I saw you last night. I knew. I
           could see it on you. I know you too well.

ALI   It wasn't what you think, Chris.

CHRIS   What about AIDS. Eh?

ALI   I know, I know . . .

CHRIS   Do you?

ALI   I was drunk . . . it all happened in a flash.

CHRIS   Funny that you were drunk. When you're out with
             me you don't drink. Suddenly, you're knocking it
             back like there's no tomorrow!

             (*Pause.*)

             Were you naked?

ALI   Don't.

CHRIS   Were you?

ALI   Yes.

CHRIS   Oh, naked?

ALI   Yes.

CHRIS   In his bed?

ALI   Yes. Don't ask all the facts Chris, please. I'm sorry, I
             thought it was over. You kept saying it was over.

CHRIS   It is now.

ALI   I feel so guilty. You make me feel so guilty.

CHRIS   Typical, typical. You did this on purpose didn't you?
             Did this to hurt me on purpose?

ALI   Love me, Chris. Love me.

CHRIS   Love you . . . I'll kill you! I'll kill him . . . I will. I'll
             kill him. I will kill that bastard, I will, and I'll kill you
             as well. God I will.

ALI   I thought you said you could cope?

CHRIS   I am coping. This is coping. This is what I call coping
             with it. I'm coping and I think I'm coping very well.

             (CHRIS *doesn't know what to do. He storms out of the
             room and slams the door.*)

ALI   Don't! Chris don't . . .

             (CHRIS *marches back into the room, with more fire
             than before.*)

CHRIS   Did you have a, did you have, you know . . . Did
             you?

ALI	It wasn't like that.
CHRIS	Did you. Did you?
ALI	No.

(CHRIS *sits*.)

CHRIS	I trusted you like I trust my own Mother.
ALI	It was hardly anything.
CHRIS	It was everything. It was everything . . .
ALI	Stop shouting at me . . .
CHRIS	(*calmer*) What am I gonna do? Eh? What am I going to do?

(CHRIS *storms out of the room once more, then returns*.)

Just answer me one thing. Just one thing. Did you touch his dick?

ALI	Chris.
CHRIS	Did you?
ALI	Don't ask me.
CHRIS	I'm asking you . . . You did. You had to. How could you not. How could she not . . . You foolish sod.

(CHRIS *walks off once more, then returns*.)

Did he?

ALI	What?
CHRIS	Did he, you know, thing? Did he? I bet he did.
ALI	No.
CHRIS	He did.
ALI	He didn't.
CHRIS	Liar.
ALI	You're insane.

CHRIS   I hate you.

ALI   I hate you.

CHRIS   Did he?

ALI   Stop it! Just stop it!

CHRIS   I must know. The whole truth from you.

ALI   Why? It'll kill you.

        (CHRIS *performs around the room.*)

CHRIS   So it started with a few drinks, and a dance. And the room is dark.

ALI   It wasn't dark.

        (CHRIS *stops in his tracks.*)

CHRIS   So it started with a few drinks, and a dance and the room is light, and then there's a feel and you feel him, and he's big and strong.

ALI   You are sick.

CHRIS   And the guards are down, and then tongues become involved, and then more rancid wine, and then more feeling, and it feels good, and you're drifting, and going further down, down, and I'm listening to some stupid programme on the World Service about Chilean nose flutes.

ALI   Look it wasn't like that. I've done it. It's over. I hated it. It wasn't anything like what you think in your imagination.

CHRIS   How do you know what I think?

ALI   I thought you didn't want me. If you do then you'll have to take responsibility for your own actions.

CHRIS   So it's my fault is it?

ALI   I can't take the questioning, Chris. I can't stand the guilt. I'm not God, Chris. If you can cope with this, good. If not, I'm sorry for you. And I'm sorry that it's over, that it's finished.

CHRIS   Just tell me one thing. Just once.

ALI	What are you getting out of it?
CHRIS	Was he better than me?
ALI	Why are you killing yourself?
CHRIS	Be honest, was he?
ALI	No.
CHRIS	Liar.
ALI	I'm not.
CHRIS	Liar!
ALI	It wasn't anything.
CHRIS	Liar.
ALI	It wasn't.
CHRIS	Liar.
ALI	I'm telling you the truth, which is more than you ever tell me.
CHRIS	Liar.
ALI	Chris?
CHRIS	Liar.
ALI	(*stops, a pause*) Alright, Alright. He was better than you. He was wonderful!
	(*A beat.*)
CHRIS	I don't believe you!
	(*Abba plays. "S.O.S.". They remain still as the lights fade.*)

Scene Five.

Day. The slopes. Higher up the slopes. A bright day. As the music fades, we see DAVE, *screaming and enjoying the skiing, come from upstage to a downstage position. He turns and looks upstage. He has become very confident on the skis.*

DAVE	(*calling upstage*) Come on . . . Come on . . . what are you doing?

(*Silence.*)

Come on, it's easy, you did it yesterday. Watch the top, it's icy. Come on.

(MEL *comes skiing onto the stage. She is wearing an outrageously lavish all-in-one tight ski suit and sunglasses. She turns, puts glasses on her head.*)

MEL	Wow, that was good.
DAVE	Did you come down the red run?
MEL	I crossed it.
DAVE	It's bad. I was going to come down it, then I chickened out, came through the trees.
MEL	Off piste.
DAVE	Off mi 'ead . . . I nearly lost it at the top.
MEL	I saw you, legs akimbo. Not very good style, Dave.
DAVE	Different anyway. Again?
MEL	Again?
DAVE	Yeah? I want to make sure I beat Chris in the slalom.
MEL	I would have thought you'd thrash him.
DAVE	Come on . . . Let's go again, it's brilliant.

(DAVE *starts to depart.*)

MEL	Let me catch my breath.
DAVE	No come on, keep it going, this'll get you fit.
MEL	What about Bev?
DAVE	What about her?
MEL	Shouldn't we go back?
DAVE	What for?
MEL	Well . . .
DAVE	No, she's okay. She knows where we are. I mean she can't join us, can she?

MEL   How is she?

DAVE   A pain.

MEL   You can't blame her for that.

DAVE   Can't I? She's a stupid bitch. I'm glad to be out of her
           way. Her voice goes through me.

MEL   Oh, she dotes on you.

DAVE   I know, it's brilliant.

MEL   Do you think you're suited?

DAVE   Who, me and Bev? Give us a break. It's something to
           do when the pub shuts innit?

MEL   You're horrible to her.

DAVE   She loves it. They all do.

MEL   So it's not serious with you and Bev?

DAVE   Not from my side it isn't. Too much of a rover.

MEL   So what's going to happen?

DAVE   Dunno.

MEL   I think Bev can hear wedding bells.

DAVE   Yeah, I hear alarm bells. I may like the simple things
           in life Melissa, but it doesn't mean I'm going to marry
           one of them.

MEL   Very witty.

DAVE   I have my moments.

MEL   Not original, though.

DAVE   Is anything? I was best man for a mate of mine about
           three years ago. I got a book on marriage speeches,
           comes in handy in moments of crisis. Load of rubbish
           really. But one of them stayed with me. "My wife
           says we only have one thing in common - we both
           love the same man". That's me. I love me, who do
           you love?

MEL   So don't you care anything for Bev?

DAVE	Hey, let's not get all serious.
MEL	Why are you with her?
DAVE	Come on, let's ski . . .
MEL	Yeah.

(*They begin to move off stage, then* DAVE *stops.*)

DAVE	You know the funny thing is, she'll probably think I'm up to no good with you.
MEL	No she won't.
DAVE	Yeah, she will.
MEL	Well, she'd be wrong.
DAVE	Would she?
MEL	Well wouldn't she?

(*Silence.*)

DAVE	A lot of things happen in my head, Mel.
MEL	Not another one?
DAVE	Yeah, I see a lot of things in my head Mel. And you're involved.
MEL	Really.
DAVE	Yeah.
MEL	I see things in my head as well, Dave.
DAVE	Oh yeah?
MEL	What do you think?
DAVE	About what?
MEL	The things you see?
DAVE	Dunno.
MEL	No?
DAVE	No.

MEL	Do you think we should do something about it?
DAVE	Depends if we're seeing the same things.
MEL	I think we should ski.
DAVE	I think we should talk for a bit.
MEL	What about Dave, we don't have a lot in common.
DAVE	Don't say that. You hardly know me.
MEL	I know your type.
DAVE	Yeah, and I know your type.
MEL	And what's that supposed to mean?
DAVE	It can mean what you want it to mean. In my head it means something really dangerous.
MEL	Really?
DAVE	You'd better watch me, Mel.
MEL	Why?
DAVE	I might take advantage of you.
MEL	I don't think so.
DAVE	I could do you some serious damage.
MEL	Is that a come-on?
DAVE	Might be.
MEL	You've got such charm.
DAVE	Like Chris?
MEL	What do you mean?
DAVE	I saw him chatting you up the other day.
MEL	Oh yeah. What's wrong, were you jealous?
DAVE	What did he say?
MEL	He told me what he'd like to do to me.
DAVE	I'd like to do the same.
MEL	Oh come on, Dave. You'd run a mile.

DAVE	I don't think that I would.
MEL	I think you're all talk Dave. You're on holiday, you can say what you like. It won't matter when you get home, it'll be back to second hand cars and Bev.
DAVE	I might not go back. I might stay here in Europe. Doss about for a bit. I've got a couple of grand on my Visa card. Bev doesn't know. Just in case anything turned up.
MEL	Like what?
DAVE	Like you, for example. I could shack up with you for a bit.
MEL	Yeah, I bet you'd like it in Paris.
DAVE	I'd like it anywhere with you.
MEL	Come here then.
DAVE	What?
MEL	I said come here.
DAVE	Eh?
MEL	Come here Dave, I want to have you now!
DAVE	(*gob-smacked*) Hang on.
MEL	Shut up and come over here.
DAVE	Are you serious?
	(DAVE *moves awkwardly over to* MELISSA. *She holds his face and kisses him full on the mouth.*)
MEL	I think you're wonderfully innocent, Dave.
	(*They kiss.* DAVE *is staggered.*)
	Is that the best you can do?
DAVE	It is with my skis on.
	(*A beat.*)
MEL	Take your skis off, then.
DAVE	Yeah! Yeah!

(*Lights, music.* DAVE *hurriedly takes off his skis.* MEL *also takes hers off. Abba's "Take A Chance On Me" plays as the lights fade.*)

Scene Six

Evening. Last night of the holiday. The lounge area of the hotel, which is decorated for a party. A few streamers, a lot of wine and steins, a table and chairs. Atmosphere informal but tetchy, everyone dressed in their best. BEV *is sat in a large chair with a cast on her ankle.* CHRIS *is already quite drunk, but it's going to get worse.* ALISON *is trying to enjoy the party.*

CHRIS   (*to* BEV) You alright Bev?

BEV   Feels okay now.

ALI   Feel better?

BEV   A bit. Happy Birthday, Chris. (*She sings "Happy Birthday To You".*)

CHRIS   Cheers, Bev.

          (BEV *hands him a present.*)

          Oh, thank you. That's very big of you. What is it? An umbrella? A three-piece suite? Double Decker bus?

ALI   What is it?

BEV   A tea towel with apfelstrudle recipes on it - it was all I could think of.

          (CHRIS *displays the tea towel.*)

ALI   Oh!

CHRIS   Thanks, Bev.

BEV   Oh, it was nothing.

CHRIS   I know that. No present from you, Al?

ALI   I didn't think you'd want one from me.

CHRIS   (*feeling* BEV'S *cast*) Does that hurt Bev? Does that? How about that?

BEV   (*screaming*) Oh, Chris . . . Ohhh, it's started throbbing again.

CHRIS   Has it?

            (DAVE *and* MELISSA *enter.* DAVE *has a number of steins with him and* MEL *has wine. She is quieter.*)

DAVE   Well done, you lucky git. I thought I had you at the end. (*Handing* CHRIS *a stein of lager.*) Get this down you. Cheers.

CHRIS   Cheers, Dave. Better luck next year. I knew when it came to the crunch I'd beat you. When you see Kevin tell him he owes me fifty pence.

MEL   You alright Bev?

BEV   Throbbing.

MEL   Just sit and relax.

BEV   Can't do much else, can I?

DAVE   I'll beat you next time.

CHRIS   Promises, promises.

BEV   Hasn't the holiday gone quick. First two days seemed to drag, and then it flashed by. Mind you, sitting inside is no fun. It's no fun, Chris.

CHRIS   No?

BEV   Back home tomorrow.

ALL   Yeah.

CHRIS   Back to reality.

BEV   Oh, we've met some really nice people haven't we Dave?

DAVE   (*acknowledging* MEL) We have.

BEV   You'll have to stay in touch Ali, when you get back. Its not far to go up North, is it babe?

DAVE   (*only half interested*) Not far. No.

BEV   Been a great first holiday, hasn't it Dave?

CHRIS   Would you come skiing again? (*Everyone laughs at this.*) How about you, Dave?

DAVE   Dunno.

CHRIS   When do you go back to reality, Melissa?

MEL   I've got nothing to rush back for. I may stay a week longer.

CHRIS   Aren't you the lucky one?

ALI   Don't have a lot to drink.

CHRIS   Eh?

DAVE   It's his birthday isn't it? Leave him.

CHRIS   Might see you back next year?

BEV   We're not coming next year.

DAVE   No.

CHRIS   No?

DAVE   Bev wants to go somewhere hot, don't you Bev?

ALI   Oh lovely.

BEV   Somewhere where I can just sit by the pool and relax.

CHRIS   That's what you've done here for two days.

BEV   You know what I mean?

CHRIS   Try Benidorm.

ALI   Yeah!

CHRIS   I think you two would like it. They serve a lot of lager and have video lounges.

DAVE   What are you on about?

CHRIS   And you can still get fish and chips. None of this foreign crap.

DAVE   You what?

CHRIS   Just a joke, Dave.

DAVE	Oh.
BEV	Sounds good Benidorm, babe.
ALI	Anyone want any more to drink?
CHRIS	Why don't you have one Ali? I'd like to see you have a drink, relax, you've been on edge all holiday.
ALI	I think you've had enough.
CHRIS	Do you?
ALI	Yes I do.
CHRIS	I don't think so. I don't think I've had nearly enough. You see I know when I've had enough. I vomit and fall over.
MEL	You really are amusing, Chris.
ALI	He's making an exhibition of himself.
DAVE	No he ain't.
CHRIS	Come on Ali, have a drink?
ALI	I don't want one.
CHRIS	Why not, can't you trust yourself?
MEL	(diverting) Bad luck today Dave, It was a close thing. I thought you were going to thrash Chris.
CHRIS	I know you did, but you were wrong, Mel.
MEL	I certainly was.
CHRIS	And I didn't even get a kiss off you for winning?
MEL	You'll get over it.
CHRIS	Will I?
BEV	Benidorm sounds nice. I'll get a brochure when we get back.
ALI	You'll find somewhere quieter on that coast Bev, if you fancy it.
CHRIS	Are you going to have a drink Al, or not?

DAVE	She doesn't like drinking when you're around, Chris. Not like the other night eh, Al? Knocking 'em back like there was no tomorrow.
CHRIS	(*surprised*) Oh yeah?
BEV	Just have a glass of wine Ali, I am. It's that Liebfraumilch, I think.
DAVE	Cramps her style.
BEV	It's nice.
ALL	Come on.
ALI	I just don't feel like a drink.
	(*Silence.*)
CHRIS	You won your medal didn't you?
ALI	So did you.
CHRIS	But you thought I wouldn't. You thought Dave would beat me didn't you. Well, you were another one who was wrong, I did it . . . Ha! I learned to ski.
ALI	I'm pleased for you.
BEV	There would have been no living with him if he'd have lost.
CHRIS	I'm a very bad loser, Bev.
BEV	So is Dave.
DAVE	Aren't we all.
CHRIS	Do you know you look radiant tonight Bev. Don't you think so Dave? Doesn't she look fantastic? Oooh Bev, I could ravish you tonight.
BEV	Chris?
CHRIS	I could honest. I could.
BEV	So what's it like being thirty three, Chris?
CHRIS	The same as being thirty two but one year older.
BEV	Half-way house?
CHRIS	And not even married?

BEV	Not even engaged.
ALI	Or ever likely to be.
CHRIS	And unlike some I could mention, untouched by human hands.
DAVE	Poor you.
CHRIS	I'll survive, Dave.
DAVE	I'm sure you will. Things'll be different at home, eh Chris? (*Meaning the affair.*)
CHRIS	I am one of life's survivors. But what about you two? Love's sweet thing and no sign of a ring, no sign of living together. I smell a split in the air?
ALI	I think we should go, Chris.
BEV	There's no split is there, babe?
ALI	I think we should go.
BEV	No, don't go, Ali!
CHRIS	I think we should wait for Tony. After all he's the one who's helped us all to ski.
ALL	Yeah!
DAVE	Come on then, Chris.
CHRIS	What?
DAVE	Tell us the big secret.
CHRIS	What secret, Dave?
DAVE	That advert you've done that you wouldn't tell us about. I reckon its for 'Do-It-All'. "How do Do-It-All do it . . ."
CHRIS	You wouldn't believe me if I told you.
BEV	Is it for Philadelphia Cheese spread?
DAVE	That's a woman.
BEV	Well it could be.
MEL	It's not for Ski yoghurt is it?

CHRIS	You're funny Melissa, did you know that?
MEL	I'm sure its something obvious.
CHRIS	No, actually its not. It's actually for P.G. tips. (*Everyone laughs at this.*) What a laugh, eh? I'm a monkey on the tea advert. A man of thirty three.
DAVE	I knew it. I knew it.
BEV	(*to* ALI) He told me that but I didn't believe him.
DAVE	I knew it.
BEV	Which monkey are you, Chris?
CHRIS	The one with the teeth.
MEL	So Ali was wrong Chris, you are famous . . .
CHRIS	(*mocking*) Ha-ha.
ALI	(*in his defence*) He only did it for the money.
DAVE	Good money, is it?
BEV	Is Tony coming?
CHRIS	Better ask Alison.
MEL	He said he'd pop in.
CHRIS	Well that'd be nice wouldn't it?
DAVE	So you're one of those dozy sods who does the voice for the monkeys?
CHRIS	That's me.
BEV	Do it, Chris, do the voice, do it.
DAVE	(*attempting the voice from the advert*) "This ain't blinkin' Calais, more like blinkin' Catford". . . "Mind your blinkin' French!"
BEV	Good that, babe.
DAVE	Good money is it?
CHRIS	It pays the rent.

BEV	What do they do Chris? Do they cast the monkeys first and fit a voice, or do they cast the voice first and cast a monkey to fit the voice?
CHRIS	I don't know, Bev.
ALI	We should go soon. I've still go to pack.
CHRIS	I think they cast the tea bag first.
ALI	I don't want to go home Chris, do you?
CHRIS	I don't want to go with you.
	(*Icy pause.*)
BEV	Where's Tony?
DAVE	Hey, do you think we should have a bit of a whip-round for him? I'm mean, he's been brilliant, hasn't he? I think he's been really brilliant.
CHRIS	Yeah, I'll write him a cheque.
BEV	How much are we all chipping in?
DAVE	Fiver each maybe? Tenner?
CHRIS	I'll give him Kevin's fifty pence.
BEV	Where is he?
CHRIS	Probably giving some extra tuition.
BEV	It's a bit dark for that, isn't it?
ALI	He was joking, Bev.
BEV	Was he? He's so funny, I can never tell.
ALI	No . . . I know . . .
CHRIS	You're very quiet, Melissa.
MEL	I was watching the show . . .
CHRIS	Listen, why don't you bore us to death with some crap about how you were mistreated at public school?
ALI	Chris!

CHRIS	You know the sort of thing, all girls in the dorms, midnight feasts, great adventures, how you secretly lusted for the matron.
ALI	Chris, have another drink and shut up!
CHRIS	Come on Mel . . .
MEL	No, I'll leave all that to you Chris.
CHRIS	All what?
MEL	Boring everyone to death.
CHRIS	Oh, I said she was funny. I didn't realise the likes of you had jokes, I thought it was all about 'sarcasm'.
MEL	You'd be surprised, Chris.
CHRIS	Go on, Mel, surprise me.
MEL	We have jokes.
CHRIS	(*mocking*) Yeah . . . Yeah. Yeah . . . oh, yeah.
MEL	We have jokes about the English abroad. Their incompetence.
CHRIS	I bet you do.
ALI	I don't think we need to get personal.
CHRIS	Don't you talk to me about getting personal.
MEL	We have some really funny jokes about the way men seduce women. What they say to them. What they would like to do to them. (*Icy.*) It's really funny, Chris.
CHRIS	Who invited you anyway?
MEL	You did.
CHRIS	No messages today, Mel? What's the husband up to, eh? (*Putting on posh accent.*) "Miss Jones, come in and take something down, will you?"
ALI	I think this has gone far enough.
CHRIS	What's it like being a snob, Melissa?

MEL	It's great. What's it like having a chip on your shoulder?
CHRIS	Have I got a chip on my shoulder?
MEL	A very big one.
CHRIS	Yes, we're frying tonight.
MEL	We certainly are.
CHRIS	You've been putting some practice in haven't you? You and Dave? You looked very cosy.
DAVE	Give it a rest, Chris.
BEV	They're only skiing together, aren't they Al?
CHRIS	Oh, right.
BEV	It was only practice, Chris.
CHRIS	Practice for what?
MEL	You know, you are the worse kind of Brit, Chris. Narrow-minded, self-centred, blinkered and pissed.
CHRIS	Oh, swear words.
MEL	And what's worse is that there is no excuse for you. You're like a spoilt brat.
CHRIS	Listen who's talking!
ALI	I think you've said about enough, Melissa.
CHRIS	Don't talk to me about England, you only live there half the bloody time. You were the one who said it was a nation of theme pubs . . .
ALI	It's shopkeepers . . .
CHRIS	Whatever . . . She's poncing about on the Rive Gauche or something and telling us how to behave.
DAVE	Give it a rest Chris, will you? You're like me, can't even manage a word of French.
CHRIS	I can. Bonjour and Merde, that's two words. Hello shit.

MEL	Don't, Dave.
DAVE	You know you've got a problem, mate.
CHRIS	Have I.
DAVE	Yeah, you have.
CHRIS	Oh have I?
MEL	Please, can we leave it?
CHRIS	You told me to keep away from her didn't you?
DAVE	You're playing with fire.
CHRIS	Better pass me the fire bucket. I think I'm going to be sick.
DAVE	Oh yeah . . . I bet you can't wait to get back, eh Chris? Back to the office.
CHRIS	No I can't.
DAVE	No right. Sounds like a good office to me. Lots of young women, they all think you're the dog's bollocks, yeah good office, Ali? Have you been?
ALI	No, I . . .
DAVE	Thought as much. Keeps you well away, eh?

(*As the temperature rises,* TONY, *wearing a pair of levis, and a smart après ski shirt enters with a stein. He is greeted with cheers from everyone. It is a release.*)

TONY	And so we are all here. Yes?
ALL	Yes . . .
TONY	The racing team. This is very good. We all have a good time. Much beer. Good time, Chris?
CHRIS	A great time Tony. A great time.
TONY	How is the leg Bev, very good?
BEV	Yeah, its fine.

TONY	I think it will be very good, when the plaster is taken away. Alison how are you, very good?
ALI	Fine thanks . . .
BEV	Dave?
DAVE	What?
BEV	If I asked you, would you get engaged to me?
DAVE	What?
BEV	Tonight.
DAVE	Eh?
BEV	Would you?
DAVE	Hang on, Bev.
BEV	Go on, babe.
DAVE	(*sharper*) Hang on.
BEV	You must know if you would?
TONY	For drinks everyone is alright for a beer?
CHRIS	I think Alison would like another, Tony.
TONY	Alison, for you another?
ALI	No thanks.
CHRIS	Didn't say that the other night.
BEV	Dave?
DAVE	Bev, shut up will you.
MEL	I think it's about time I turned in.
DAVE	Not yet. Stay for another.
BEV	Dave?
DAVE	Just have another drink.
BEV	What about me, ask me?
DAVE	Do you want another drink, Bev?
MEL	I should go, really.

DAVE   No. Stay.

TONY   Melissa, stay, please.

CHRIS   (*obtuse*) You don't wear pyjamas Tony, do you?

TONY   I don't understand.

ALI   You said you'd leave it.

CHRIS   Don't believe a word I say.

MEL   No. I really should go. I'd like to be up early
            tomorrow.

CHRIS   Wouldn't we all, Melissa?

DAVE   I'll see you later, shall I?

MEL   That's up to you.

TONY   Please not to go. Stay, enjoy.

MEL   No. I'm going.

CHRIS   Melissa, the party's just starting.

MEL   That's why I'm going, Chris.

BEV   (*loud*) Dave do you want to get engaged or what?

CHRIS   Yes, you go to bed. I'll be up in a minute.

BEV   Dave?

DAVE   Just back off a bit, Bev.

BEV   Eh?

MEL   I'll see you tomorrow.

            (MEL *makes to leave*.)

DAVE   Hang on, I want to talk to you.

MEL   Not now.

BEV   Talk, talk what about?

TONY   Please . . . we have good time . . .

MEL   Good night. Night.

            (MEL *exits*. DAVE *tries to follow, can't, calls after her*.)

BEV	Babe?
DAVE	I'll see you later.
BEV	Dave, I think you should explain what's going on.
DAVE	Shut up, you silly bitch. Just shut up.
CHRIS	Looks like you've got too much on your plate, Dave.
DAVE	And you'd know, wouldn't you?
BEV	Dave, listen to me.
DAVE	Why?
CHRIS	Are you going to show us the knees up, Tony?
TONY	I am sorry.
CHRIS	You will be.
ALI	Shall we go?
BEV	I think I'll come with you, Al.
CHRIS	You know the knees up, slap thighs here comes Cadbury's.
TONY	Tyrolean dance. Ah, not for me. I am better at the dirty dancing.
CHRIS	Why don't you and Al have a dance?
ALI	Why don't you leave it out?
BEV	Can we talk please, Dave?
TONY	I think Chris is enjoying the beer. It is strong, yes?
ALI	Let's go Chris.
CHRIS	How many do you get through in one season, eh Tony?
ALI	Let's go.
TONY	What?
CHRIS	Feel good did it?
TONY	I do not understand you Chris.

CHRIS   You bastard.

TONY   I'm sorry I can't understand.

CHRIS   Don't give me that.

BEV   What's happening here, we're supposed to be having a good time.

CHRIS   You?

TONY   Yes?

CHRIS   You?

DAVE   He's had too much. Can't take the ale. Come on Mr Shifter, don't make a scene. Do you know the piano's on my foot?

CHRIS   (*staring at* TONY) You?

DAVE   You hum it son, I'll play it.

ALI   Chris, I'm going.

CHRIS   You shit.

BEV   Shall we dance anybody?

CHRIS   I want you outside.

TONY   Outside it is cold.

CHRIS   I want you outside now.

           (CHRIS *and* TONY *are squaring up. It is uncomfortable.* CHRIS *is more the aggressor, but he is frightened.* DAVE *steps in - it's all getting ugly.*)

DAVE   Hey, come on, Chris. Leave him. He hasn't done anything.

CHRIS   Hasn't he, he knows he has. I'll kill you. I'll kill you.

TONY   I do not think so.

CHRIS   I'll have you.

           (ALI *comes to* CHRIS *to restrain him.*)

ALI   Chris leave it, leave it you're not a fighter, leave it, its nothing.

CHRIS	I'll kill you, I will. I will kill you.
TONY	(*rising to the bait*) You think you are good? I don't think you are too good. I will beat you at anything. I will beat you anytime.
CHRIS	I'll beat you at anything.
TONY	I don't think you are too good.
CHRIS	Yeah?
TONY	Yes.
CHRIS	Yeah?
TONY	Yes.
ALI	Chris, leave it now, its not worth it. (*She holds him.*)
CHRIS	Get off me or I'll kill you as well.
TONY	I think you have a problem, Chris.
ALI	Chris, just cool off.
TONY	Your English women, they are all the same. As if they have never been out of your country. Their men cannot ski so good, so I show them a good time. This says a lot about the English I think.
CHRIS	(*screaming*) I'll have you, mate.
TONY	I do not think this is so.
CHRIS	I'll beat you at anything.
ALI	Oh, for God's sake!
TONY	Anything? Okay so tomorrow morning we will ski down the Gwanschoff?
DAVE	Hey come on, leave it . . .
CHRIS	Anything.
TONY	I joke with you, you will not do this.
CHRIS	You go anywhere near Alison again and I'll slit your throat and I mean it.
ALI	We're going home tomorrow anyway.

CHRIS   I mean it.

TONY   You are a crazy man, Chris.

CHRIS   (*insane*) Am I? Am I?

BEV   (*can't fathom it*) Is he drunk? He must be. Is he
            drunk Al?

ALI   Chris, get your things. Let's go.

CHRIS   No . . . No I mean it. Tomorrow, right. I'll race you. I
            ought to batter your brains in but I'll play you at your
            own game. I'll wait by the cable car.

ALI   This is stupid.

DAVE   You'll break your bleeding neck.

CHRIS   I won't.

DAVE   You can only do a snowplough.

CHRIS   I beat you in the slalom, didn't I?

DAVE   Only 'cos I let you.

CHRIS   (*shocked*) You didn't, did you?

TONY   (*for the first time a real menace*) You are like your
            football team, in the head not too good. I cannot let
            you ski the Gwanschoff, you will be killed maybe.
            For your pride I understand, we have pride, too. But
            life must go on. A night with Alison is nothing for me,
            a 'good time' perhaps. She is not for me.

ALI   Chris, let's be reasonable people.

CHRIS   I'll meet you at half eight tomorrow.

ALI   Chris, we fly at twelve.

CHRIS   Shut up you.

TONY   What do I have to prove, I will not be there. You
            see Chris, you cannot understand how easy it is for
            me. I can pick up the girls, I can ski the mountain, I
            am very good, but you, what can you do? You are a
            voice of a berry. You are an old man I think.

CHRIS   I'm thirty three, that's not even middle-aged.

(*A beat.*)

BEV   It is.

TONY   You must water your own garden, Chris. Otherwise your garden will be very dry.

CHRIS (*dead straight*) You be there tomorrow.

TONY   Okay. And if you are very lucky you will only break one leg. (*He turns to leave.*) Good bye Alison. Have a good life, on your own.

(TONY *exits.*)

DAVE   You'll never get down that mountain in one piece.

CHRIS Want to bet?

DAVE   A hundred quid.

CHRIS Right. Right.

(*Silence.*)

Right. (*A beat.*) I'm going to bed. Don't wake me up, if you come back.

(CHRIS *exits in silence.*)

BEV   I think me and you have to have a long and serious talk, David. I don't like what's been going on, to be honest. I think we need to sort things out, otherwise I think I'll have to finish it.

DAVE   That's what you think is it?

BEV   I don't want to but I might have to.

DAVE   Good.

BEV   Why, do you want to?

DAVE   Yeah, I do.

ALI   Look, don't you two start arguing, for God's sake. It'll all be over tomorrow, we'll be on the plane laughing about it.

BEV   I don't think I'll be laughing much.

ALI   Everyone's had too much to drink. It always happens.

DAVE	I haven't had too much, I haven't had enough to drink.
BEV	Well I think you have.
DAVE	Well what do you know? I'm going to bed.
BEV	Can we talk?
DAVE	Not now.
BEV	Can we talk now, please?
DAVE	Talk?
BEV	Yes.
DAVE	That's all you ever do, talk, talk, talk - you're like a bleeding parrot . . . And the amazing thing is that you don't say anything. And that voice, oh my God, what a voice . . . that squeaky high voice. It goes through me. Babe, babe, babe, Dave, Dave, Dave, Kevin, Kevin . . . sometimes you don't stop to take a breath. No wonder you've got a weak chest. Why should I talk to you Bev, you never say anything interesting. In all the time I've known you you've never spoken a single sentence that has made any sense. You're thick.
BEV	Oh am I, well that's news to me.
DAVE	See? See? You stupid cow.
BEV	I'm not going to stand here and take all this. Not from you, not from anyone.
DAVE	Well hop it then, Bev. I'm going upstairs. So shove that up your arse.

(DAVE *exits*. BEV *cannot move*.)

BEV	Dave, I haven't finished talking to you . . . I bet he's going to see her. I knew there was something going on. He said there wasn't but I knew it. The other day when he came back I could smell her perfume on him, she wears a lot of that Fendi, I can't wear that it makes my skin come up, I can only wear Clarins. I mean, I don't know a lot about skiing, but I know you don't have to get so close. Do you know I wish I was stronger. I wish I was stronger with men. I wish I could just love 'em and leave 'em. I can't though. I'm

pathetic with men. I mean, I'm still writing to that one in Greece . . . I'm a softy.

ALI   No you're not, Bev. You're just like us all. Insecure. Chris could be killed on that mountain tomorrow and I wouldn't have a thing.

BEV   He won't seriously do it, will he?

ALI   Yeah he will, because half the time he doesn't know what's real and what's fantasy.

BEV   What about you and Tony, was that real?

ALI   Yes, that was real.

(*A beat.*)

BEV   What was it like?

(*A beat.*)

ALI   It was good. No, no . . . in fact it was more than good, it was exciting because it was different, and because I knew it was wrong. I knew exactly what Tony was after. I was after it more than he was. I told Chris that we did nothing . . . but we did everything . . .

BEV   What!

ALI   . . . and it was fantastic!

(*Abba plays as the lights fade.*)

Scene Seven

Early the next morning on the slopes outside the hotel. A crisp, dry day. DAVE *is sorting out some ski gear.* BEV, *with her crutch and a bag full of presents, comes onto the stage. She calls from off stage, but* DAVE *doesn't respond.*

BEV   (*voice off*) Dave? Dave? . . . Dave?

DAVE   (*mocks*) Dave, Dave . . .

BEV   (*enters*) Dave, are you ready?

(*No response.*)

The bus is ready, we're all packed. Dave?

(*No response.*)

Babe? Kevin, come on now you naughty boy, Aunty Bev's let you play out this morning and now its time to go home. Kevin come on!

DAVE   (*dead*) There's no need to shout.

BEV   Better go, babe.

DAVE   I'm er . . . not going back, Bev.

BEV   Eh?

DAVE   I'm not coming.

BEV   What do you mean?

DAVE   (*mocks*) What do you mean? I mean I'm staying here.

BEV   Eh?

DAVE   Yeah.

BEV   (*seeing a potential game*) Well, let Kevin come back and we'll get him on the coach.

DAVE   (*ice*) Kevin's dead, Bev.

BEV   (*not believing*) He isn't?

DAVE   He is. (*A beat.*) He died in a nasty accident.

BEV   I don't understand you, babe.

DAVE   A reindeer ran him over.

BEV   This is serious Dave.

DAVE   It was serious for Kev, cut his head clean off.

BEV   Be serious.

DAVE   I'm staying here. You go back. England's a cesspit compared to this.

BEV   It's home.

DAVE   Was.

BEV   Right.

DAVE   Sorry.

BEV   But . . .

DAVE   Look . . . I told you not to get involved, Bev. I've got
           to do it.

BEV   What about, me?

DAVE   What about you? We had a good time. It was never
           going to last, was it? Did you think it would?

BEV   Are you with her?

DAVE   What does it matter?

BEV   It matters.

DAVE   Yeah, I am for the time being, but it won't last, I know
           that. It's a change, innit?

BEV   (*very upset*) I thought you loved me, I thought you
           were right for me.

DAVE   I'm not right for anybody yet.

BEV   What about the presents?

DAVE   Keep 'em.

BEV   I don't believe you Dave, you're joking aren't you?

DAVE   No. Keep 'em.

BEV   Don't joke, Dave.

DAVE   I don't mean to hurt you love, but it's every man for
           himself. I'm a bastard. You must think I'm a real shit.

BEV   (*composure*) No, you're not a shit Dave. You're not a
           real shit. You're a fart, a shit's too good for you. (*She
           starts to leave.*)

           (ALI *has entered upstage with two cases. She sees*
           BEV.)

ALI   Is the bus ready, Bev?

BEV   Yeah. Yeah it is.

           (BEV *hobbles* . . . DAVE *stands alone, then exits
           downstage right.*)

DAVE   See you both . . . take care . . .

             (BEV *is in tears.* ALI *comes down to her.*)

ALI   Are you okay?

BEV   (*crying*) No.

ALI   What's happened?

BEV   Nothing. I'll see you on the coach.

             (*As* BEV *hobbles off downstage left.* CHRIS *enters upstage right. He is freezing. He is wearing his ski gear, having just returned from the mountain.*)

ALI   It's ten past nine. The bus leaves in ten minutes. Are you coming or are you staying as well?

CHRIS   I'm coming.

ALI   I take it Tony didn't appear?

CHRIS   No. He didn't.

ALI   Did you think he would?

CHRIS   I thought he might at least honour his word.

ALI   He had nothing to prove.

CHRIS   Unlike you.

ALI   Come on. (*Makes to move.*)

CHRIS   Ali?

ALI   What?

CHRIS   I'm really sorry.

ALI   For what? The last ten years or the last seven days, which?

CHRIS   I think we should get married.

ALI   (*lightly*) What?

CHRIS   I'll change, I will, Al. I like looking in Marks and Spencer, I do, honest.

ALI   Don't turn everything into a joke.

CHRIS   I'll learn to cook, I'll do the washing, I'll iron all your clothes, not just the square bits.

ALI   I don't think you will. I don't want them ruining.

CHRIS   I'll never look at another woman Al, never, I promise. I want you back.

(*Silence.*)

ALI   But the thing is, Chris, do I want you back?

(*Silence.*)

CHRIS   Well, do you? (*She begins to leave.*) Ali . . . (*A beat.*) Do you . . .

(ALI *turns to go.* CHRIS *picks up his case and follows her offstage. As they leave,* TONY *enters on skis and skis downstage. He stops with a flourish and finally flicks a ski into his hands.*)

TONY   (*to the audience*) Ar, so the snow is here, you have brought the snow with you? Yes, this is very good. You all stay at the Seefelderhoff? Very good. You ski with Tony, he will show you some very good skiing, and then the sauna, very sexy. You are English yes? I like the English in Europe so very much. They come and we have a good time. Welcome to Austria!

(*A final flourish. Abba plays, "Dancing Queen".*)

Blackout.